WAR WOUNDS

DEVELOPMENT COSTS OF CONFLICT IN SOUTHERN SUDAN

by

Abdul Rahman Abu Zayd Ahmed
Beatrice Khamisa Baya
Cole P. Dodge
Oliver Meru Duku
Patricio Abibo Fully
Samuel Gonda
Marcello Lado Jada
Thomas P. Kedini
Peter van Krieken
Priscilla Kuch
Kosti Manibe
Bona Malwal
William Mogga
Siddiq Abdel Rahman Ib
Suleiman Baldo
Alfred Logune Taban
Mary Wani
Mike Wooldridge

*

Preface by Olusegun Obasanjo

Edited by Nigel Twose and Benjamin Pogrund

THE PANOS INSTITUTE
London — Paris — Washington

Published by Panos Publications Ltd
8 Alfred Place
London WC1E 7EB
UK

First published 1988

British Library Cataloguing in Publication data:
War Wounds: Sudanese people report on their war: development costs of conflict in southern Sudan.
1. Sudan. Economic development. Effects of civil wars
I. Zeid, Abu
330.9624'04

ISBN 1-870670-08-6

Arabic edition, first published 1988
ISBN 1-870670-09-4

The Panos Institute is an international information and policy studies institute, dedicated to working in partnership with others towards greater public understanding of sustainable development. Panos has offices in London, Paris and Washington DC, and was founded in 1986 by the staff of Earthscan, which had undertaken similar work since 1975.

For more information about Panos contact:
James Deane, Press Officer

Production: Jacqueline Walkden
Photo research: Patricia Lee
Cover design: Robert Purnell
Maps: Philip Davies

Printed in Great Britain by Lithoimage Ltd Nottingham.

WAR WOUNDS

DEVELOPMENT COSTS OF CONFLICT IN SOUTHERN SUDAN

SUDANESE PEOPLE REPORT ON THEIR WAR

War Wounds is part of the Panos Sahel Programme which is supported by the Danish International Development Agency (DANIDA), The Netherlands Ministry of Foreign Affairs and Oxfam UK.

The preparation, publication and dissemination of *War Wounds* is supported by:

CAFOD, Christian Aid, the Commission of the European Communities, Danchurch Aid, Deutscher Caritasverband, The National Gypsum Company of Saudi Arabia, Norwegian Church Aid, Save the Children Fund (UK), the Scottish Catholic International Aid Fund, UNICEF, USA for Africa and War on Want.

There have been many advisors to this book throughout its preparation. Most of them would prefer not to be mentioned by name: our thanks to them all.

War Wounds is dedicated to the millions of Sudanese people whose struggle to survive has been made so much harder by this war.

Jeremy Hartley/Panos Pictures

THE FLOODS AND THE WAR

On 4 August 1988, torrential rains fell on the Sudanese capital of Khartoum. Within hours, three quarters of the city was under water, and an estimated million people had been made homeless.

Such disasters rarely have a uniform impact: they target the poorest and the most vulnerable. Hardest hit by the Khartoum floodwaters were more than a million refugees, who had been displaced from southern Sudan by civil war, and were surviving in makeshift shelters around the city.

Misery on this scale, when it occurs in a major capital with a functioning airport, becomes a media event on TV screens and newspapers across the world. But those dispossessed refugees, whose miserable homes had vanished under the rising waters, were only the visible fraction of a far larger and longer-running tragedy: the war in Sudan's southern provinces, which has been raging largely unnoticed for well over 20 years, far from reporters or TV crews.

In *War Wounds*, some of the people affected by this protracted and brutal conflict speak for themselves. The picture they draw emerges in this book slowly and cumulatively: burned villages, armies and guerrillas and soldiers of fortune, deserted schools, hospitals abandoned, children trained in killing and torture, refugees scattered to neighbouring countries, cattle herds destroyed, roads sown with land mines, farmland lost to the bush. The dead are uncounted, and probably uncountable.

In late 1987, The Panos Institute had started to work with

people's organisations and the media right across the Sahel, from Senegal and Cape Verde to Ethiopia and Somalia, helping them to describe and analyse their own development experience. Our friends in the Sudan all urged that our efforts there should initially concentrate on the biggest development crisis facing that country: the war. For until this conflict in the south is honourably resolved, sustained development for the Sudan as a whole will remain a dream.

War Wounds, which is also appearing in Arabic, describes some of the development consequences of this long and bitter conflict: on livestock, farmland, forests and other natural resources; on health care, education, transport and markets; and above all, on the people. The massive influx of refugees into the north has in recent months brought the consequences of a previously hidden war to the doorsteps of northerners.

This Panos book does not take sides, nor does it offer any political solutions. General Olusegun Obasanjo, who as Nigeria's head of state, helped guide his own nation's recovery from the Biafran civil war, has contributed an important foreword, and Panos has added a chronology of historical events for non-Sudanese readers.

In Sudan today, especially in the south, communications are not easy. Even in Khartoum, telephone and telex lines are frequently down; in the south, mail rarely reaches the regional capital of Juba, and letters elsewhere disappear completely unless carried by hand. So collecting together this book has not been easy. But the difficulties experienced by Panos pale into insignificance compared to the problems our writers have faced, most of them assembling their material in the middle of civil war.

Almost all this book's 20-odd contributors are Sudanese. They vary in their political, ethnic and religious backgrounds, but all are men and women of the highest integrity, and Panos has sought corroboration of their facts and allegations. We and our Sudanese colleagues have checked and double-checked as far as is possible in such unsettled conditions. Most chapters had to be edited to avoid repetition, and time and logistics prevented taking the edited texts back to the authors for their final approval. So the responsibility for any errors or omissions belongs with Panos, and not with the original authors.

This is not a definitive account of what this terrible conflict is doing to the peoples of the Sudan. When peace has returned, such a book may one day be written. But *War Wounds* is probably the first coherent attempt to document the impacts of over two decades of vicious turmoil.

The August 1988 floods pushed a forgotten war into the international headlines. In *War Wounds*, some of those who have been involved describe some of its effects and underlying causes.

Jon Tinker
President
The Panos Institute

London
September 1988

Throughout the book, all amounts in Sudanese pounds are accompanied by an approximate US dollar conversion based on £S4 = US$1

CONTENTS

PREFACE

OLUSEGUN OBASANJO

General Olusegun Obasanjo was Nigerian Head of State from 1975 – 1979. He served as co-chairman of the 1986 Commonwealth Eminent Persons Group to promote dialogue between the South African Government and representatives of the black majority. He is a member of the InterAction Council, made up of former heads of state and prime ministers, to consider world issues. Since 1987, General Obasanjo has been actively involved in negotiations for peace in Sudan.

The civil war in the Sudan has now been in progress with varying intensity for the greater part of the three decades since the country achieved independence in January 1956. Yet, of the contemporary world's inter-communal conflicts, the Sudanese civil war is probably the least reported. Indeed, in terms of media coverage and concerned international interest, it seems a forgotten war.

It is this grievous neglect that makes the publication of this book long overdue and therefore all the more welcome. Its primary purpose is to reveal for the inspection of the world the unfolding but largely unpublicised tragedy of the Sudan in the hope that the exposed wounds of the war will concentrate minds and lead to its early end.

This book is of necessity an interim assessment of the consequences of the conflict. The full and final audit of the war will be some time coming. Even so, what is presented here must rank as one of the grimmest accounts of human suffering to emerge from a war situation anywhere in recent history.

In large parts of the south, the theatre of the war, civil society has practically disintegrated. Whole villages have been burnt and razed to the ground, agriculture abandoned, and schools, hospitals, community health centres, transport and other infrastructure destroyed.

The death toll is now estimated in millions, the first million mark having been reached as long ago as 1972.

And, typically, there is a growing refugee problem of dramatic proportions. Hundreds of thousands of refugees from the south are living in squatter camps on the outskirts of the major urban centres of Sudan, with many more in other camps in the neighbouring countries. In Ethiopia, itself hardly in a position to absorb refugees, there are some 300,000 Sudanese refugees.

Also because of the war, all major development projects in the south are at a standstill, further consolidating the economic backwardness of what is otherwise a region rich in natural resources.

But if the socio-economic devastations of the war are most pronounced in the south, they are no longer confined to that region alone. Increasingly the north, too, is now beginning to experience the direct effects of the war.

Such, in broad outline, are the lineaments of the tragedy in the making in the Sudan which *War Wounds* is at pains to bring to the attention of sentient humanity.

The book is particularly well qualified to evoke the desired response from the international community. Unlike most books in the genre, it is not the work of an enterprising journalist based on second-hand accounts obtained during a fleeting visit to the country. Neither is it the work of a self-serving politician with an eye to the main chance.

Its central merit lies in the fact that it is the direct testimony of the victims of the war themselves, coadjuted by the evidence of those who have worked alongside them over the years in the effort to alleviate their condition. *War Wounds* therefore speaks to the world with unrivalled authority and authenticity.

Yet, the book is more than a documentary account of the suffering of the Sudanese people. Perhaps more importantly, it is also an appeal, a *cri de coeur* of an embattled people for assistance not only to weather the ravages and scarcities of war, but to end the war itself and the indignities attendant upon it. The appeal is also addressed to humanity at large but, clearly, if it is to be effective it will need to register a clarion ring with the political leadership of the Sudan, in whose hands the power to end the conflict ultimately lies.

To this end, the passage of time has usefully clarified a number of points about the nature of the conflict. No one, I believe, now seriously contends that the war is a confessional conflict in the old sense of the immiscibility of Christianity and Islam. Neither is it primarily the result of an external conspiracy against the integrity of the Sudan. Equally clear, too, is the fact that the conflict cannot be resolved by arms.

As in most civil conflicts, the causes are ultimately endogenous, with deep roots in Sudanese history, from which it follows that only a political settlement, taking into account the legitimate aspirations of all sections of Sudanese society, will guarantee lasting peace.

If the harrowing revelations of this book impel all the parties to the conflict to summon the necessary political resolve to end the war, it will have served its purpose.

Clearly, after so many years of conflict, there can be no minimising the difficulties to a lasting peace. But given the will to peace, there should be no forbidding passes to an honourable settlement. It is my fervent hope that the leaders of the Sudan will prove themselves equal to the challenge of this book.

Abeokuta, Nigeria
August 1988

LIBYA
EGYPT
CHAD
Nile
Khartoum
White Nile
Blue Nile
SUDAN
Bahr el Ghazal
Upper Nile
Equatoria
ETHIOPI
CENTRAL AFRICAN REPUBLIC
ZAIRE
UGANDA
KENY
National boundary
Southern regional boundari
Jonglei Canal (construction suspended)
Riv
Main road (surfaced)
400 km

WHY THE VIOLENCE?

ABDUL RAHMAN ABU ZAYD AHMED

Professor Abdul Rahman Abu Zayd Ahmed was one of the founders and eventually Vice-Chancellor of the University of Juba. From 1976-1982, he was deeply involved, not only with educational developments in the south, but also with the major political events and leaders of the time. He went on to become Secretary-General of the National Council for Higher Education, and in 1985 took up his current position as Vice-Chancellor of Omdurman Ahlia University.

Within the pages of *War Wounds*, the reader will find personal testimonials by individuals who are keen observers of the present situation in southern Sudan. Their statements are a witness to the tragic results of a conflict which has divided our country for the second time in the span of three decades.

In order to understand correctly the background and parameters of this crisis and hence to address it with appropriate measures, certain fallacies and misleading perceptions must be put to rest.

Many a northern Sudanese, including politicians and informed writers, will tell you that the problem in southern Sudan is not one of race or religious bias, but one of sinister international interference (the Arabic word "mustahdaf" — targeted — is used daily to prove that Sudan is an object of external ill-intent). The claim is not shared by most southern Sudanese who see the conflict primarily in racial and religious terms.

This view of the conflict coloured the entire literature of the first Anya-Nya movement in the 1960s and early-1970s. The Sudan People's Liberation Movement (SPLM) now merely presents a new articulation of the same ideas about the conflict.

For example, a major obstacle to the holding of the pivotal Constitutional Conference, which is supposed to resolve the issues raised by the civil wars, has been the southerners' demand to repeal what are known as the September laws. These are Islamic or Sharia laws which were implemented in 1983 under the former president, Jafaar Nimeiri.

The Koka Dam Agreement, which was formulated in 1986 during a meeting in Ethiopia between the SPLM and the Alliance of Popular Forces, stipulates the abrogation of the September laws as a prerequisite for holding the Constitutional Conference. The leadership of the SPLM continuously refer to the existence of Sharia law as the principal reason why they cannot attend any such conference.

In July 1988, the present government — a coalition of the Umma and Democratic Unionist parties and the National Islamic Front — presented to the nation a set of what are known as "alternative laws". This legislation, in fact, is no improvement on the most controversial aspects of the Sharia laws of Nimeiri. The entire argument about the Constitutional Conference has now been firmly placed within the discussion about these alternative laws.

My point is that the religious aspect of the conflict is not one of mere claims and counterclaims, but an immediate and empirical problem, since the laws now being enacted by the central government impinge on the state structures and the constitutional framework of the nation, as well as on the economic, philosophical, intellectual, spiritual and emotional realities which both influence and are influenced by these proposed statutes.

The racial factor

The racial character of the conflict is harder to deal with, since this is an emotional charge where an individual or group of individuals may feel (and in fact, may be) discriminated against in extra-legal ways. It is true that, prior to 1983, nowhere in Sudan were citizens deprived of their constitutional, legal or human rights only because they belonged to a particular religious or ethnic group.

There were indeed controversial laws which denied all Sudanese certain legal rights. But these were an expedient carry-over from colonial days and they were applied universally — regardless of race, religion or geographic origin.

Legal guarantees or proscriptions do not, however, guarantee that individuals will not be discriminated against in other, hard to document ways. Indeed, certain practices and policies which were implemented in southern Sudan since independence could be construed as motivated to deny southerners certain rightful entitlements. As well, there are numerous areas in national life where southerners are denied privilege and access on the basis of their ethnic and geographic origin.

This point does not require belabouring because once the feeling of discrimination sets in, it acquires a reality of its own. One must admit that Sudanese society is largely a rural, tribal society, displaying certain traditional biases which are a result of the exclusivity and ethnocentrism "normal" in all groups.

A feeling of racial superiority or of being the repository of lofty social and religious values might find expression in negative and condescending attitudes towards those who are not members of the group. These are oft-observed and well-documented sociological and psychological phenomena.

One need only recall the accusations brought by a prominent Equatorian politician in the early-1980s against the Dinka when debates were going on about whether to divide the southern Sudan into three regions. The Dinka were described as an arrogant, elitist, domineering, racially biased group of people bent on enslaving all other southern Sudanese ethnic groups.

Most northern Sudanese groups are guilty of these traditional prejudices among themselves as well. Even educated Sudanese who have been exposed to the outside world and who have lived and studied in highly sophisticated environments are not free of these feelings, no matter what their ethnic background.

The basic cause

My contention is that racial and religious factors are genuine problems in the struggle to build a unified Sudanese nation, but they are not the basic cause of the present civil war. Let us move on then

Peter Charlesworth/Panos Pictures

"The only hope is for all regions to work together for the good of the country as a whole."

to address the more profound reason why differences, common to many societies, have been exaggerated to the point where violence became the chosen method of conflict response and resolution.

I believe the war, seen objectively, must be attributed primarily to comparative underdevelopment. The lack of development in the south gives rise to numerous and legitimate complaints. The southern Sudan has not received its fair share of development resources or attention, either under colonial rule or since independence.

Various reasons given for this state of affairs are not convincing, because southern Sudan is rich in resources which require only determined efforts to utilise them for the benefit of the people of the area and the entire nation. The need for the whole country to develop and share all available resources was made dramatically clear by the recent drought and famine in northern Sudan.

As the next century approaches, and as water resources and the cultivable land mass of northern Sudan shrink through drought and desertification, the only hope for the nation is for all regions to work together to exploit their particular resources for the good of the country as a whole. Yet, valuable time and treasure have been wasted for many years by neglecting the regions outside the north-central Nile Valley.

The result of erratic, ignorant and frivolous or unimplemented policies is the present poverty and misery of the entire Sudanese people.

Although the cities, towns and villages of northern Sudan are not exactly models of development, the cities and towns and villages of southern Sudan have deteriorated to the point where they are practically unsuitable for habitation. Even the capital cities of the three southern regions are suffering in an appalling manner.

Carlos Guarita/ Save the Children

"Khartoum transformed into a nightmare of squalor."

The most basic services such as health, education, security and food are in short supply during the best of times. Two civil wars have devastated the southern infrastructure with massive dislocation of populations and the attendant problems of disease, malnutrition and psychological devastation, particularly of children and young people whose physical and mental development may be permanently stunted by their experiences and lack of essential elements for growth.

Whole areas of southern Sudan have been depopulated. Southerners have had to cross international borders or move to northern Sudan. These forcible migrations have caused profound stress to the social fabric of the nation and the groups of people involved.

The capital city of Khartoum has been transformed into a nightmare of squalor, crime and insecurity; everyone in Sudan must cope with shortages of essential commodities and lack of services with the result that caring families have turned their backs on all governmental institutions, be they hospitals, schools or post offices. The government takes money for services that are not rendered, or rendered in such a way as if calculated to inflict the most anxiety on the users.

Khartoum now is reminiscent of medieval towns which one sees in Hollywood films or reads about in literature.

Underdevelopment — the norm

The question of underdevelopment is not unique to southern Sudan alone as this is the norm everywhere in the country. The northern region (or Darfur or Kordofan or Red Sea province) of Sudan can be compared to the most underdeveloped parts of the south; indeed, most regions, if left alone to traditional ways and means, would be better off than they have been under any government which has ruled the Sudan. The tragedy today is that the fate of these regions is being further disturbed by the present democratically-elected government.

There is yet another factor which must be considered if the ravages of war are not to affect our country repeatedly. Southern Sudan will not be developed as a result of concluding the present civil war or under threat of a future civil war. The proposed Constitutional Conference may produce a fine-sounding agenda for restructuring the government to grant more autonomy and a fairer distribution of power and resources to the regions, among other proposals. This will all be meaningless, however, if the present political parties continue to function as they have for the past 30 odd years.

Unfortunately, traditional loyalties and traditional leaders may be expected to continue to play a significant role in Sudan's politics. After a major, and potentially watershed, upheaval — the 1985 Uprising — romantics painted a picture of a Sudan released from traditional party structures; of instant development; of a civil service free from corruption; of an economic structure that would be capable of dealing with the masses' economic needs and of eliminating the international debt; of guaranteed human rights for all; of a democratic system of government where nobody would be denied justice; and, finally, of a Constitutional Conference that would end the civil war, chart a new way for the Sudan, settle the question of national identity and solve the state/religion dichotomy.

Three years after this major event in Sudanese history, none of these promises has been kept; instead the ordinary person is much worse off economically, corruption is still rampant and increasing and the imminent theocratisation of the state is about to put a seal on the final fragmentation of our country.

The bankruptcy of both northern and southern political parties demonstrates that they are not willing or able to deal with the primary economic problems, but are interested only in political power for self-aggrandisement and personal enrichment.

The present government of the Sudan is obviously not interested in a Constitutional Conference that will end the civil war, or they would not be pressing at this time for the implementation of Sharia law. Equally, the SPLM cannot be interested in a Constitutional Conference because they have refused to take advantage of valuable opportunities which would have denied the Islamic fundamentalists the role they enjoy now.

The SPLM did not appreciate the power and organisational

abilities of the Islamic fundamentalists, just as they placed too much confidence in the power of the Popular Alliance to implement policies and influence situations. They also appear to have misjudged the present rulers of the Sudan. The SPLM must bear their share of the historical responsibility for the state of affairs in which we find ourselves today.

Instead of dealing with the crucial issues in Sudan, namely the civil war and the economy, the government busies itself with superficial and irrelevant matters which realise no benefit (or, on the contrary, are positively detrimental) to the welfare of the majority. Simply put, the government is not serious.

We are aware of contradictions in our own description which, indeed, reflect the contradictions pervading the strategy and policies of the present coalition government. The deep incongruities within the coalition parties and among other parties are major reasons for paralysis in decision making and the total absence of action taken by government.

Dealing with the problems

How does this explanation of why we are in the present dilemma help us deal with the problem as a whole and the immediate problems of affected individuals and populations?

There must be an honest acceptance of Sudan as a sum of complex, conflicting elements.

The Government must be restructured so that the principles of a democratic system are guaranteed; namely, pluralism, basic human rights for all, equality before the law and in all national endeavours. All regions must have equal opportunity to develop. There must be a national acknowledgement that the south (and other neglected regions) represent a future source of wealth for the nation since their manpower, water, land and forests are vitally needed for the development of the nation as a whole.

All regions of the Sudan must be open to all people of the Sudan with full rights of residence, work and acquisition of property, as well as equality of opportunity with the indigenous people of the region. The national wealth must be distributed equitably. Resources of every region must be developed according to an

Thor Ullerø/Norwegian Church Aid

"We have destroyed immense wealth, lost valuable opportunities for growth and inflicted permanent injury to the national psyche, with nothing to show for our deeds."

agreed national agenda and available to all citizens, no matter from where they come.

Cultural and linguistic characteristics of every region should receive equal attention and encouragement by the relevant government institutions and private organisations. The educational system should be uniform throughout the country in its major ingredients, with allowance for regional variations. Proportional representation in the national institutions must be guaranteed.

A great deal of discussion has taken place about the question of Sudanese identity. Unfortunately, this is an issue like the other issues crucial to national harmony, which requires sensitive and imaginative handling. The acculturation process is one of historical, spiritual and emotional dimensions, and the question of identity is intimately related to that process. We cannot hope to decree a feeling of "Sudanese-ness" even if there is a national consensus on the need for a unified Sudanese identity. This can only be achieved through a long process of education, which should not overlook the advantage of maintaining diversity within unity.

The importance of initiating the long process of acquisition of a national identity is not to eliminate differences, but to ensure that those differences are not the occasion for discrimination and do not lead to violent conflict; they should rather serve to promote integration by giving various groups confidence in one another and enriching the individual Sudanese and the Sudanese society and nation.

In three decades the Sudan has lived through two tragic civil wars. We are now more than a match for the Lebanese and the Irish. During these wars we have destroyed immense wealth, lost valuable opportunities for growth, and inflicted permanent injury to the national psyche with nothing to show for our deeds.

The present civil war, however, is different from the one that preceded it. It is more sinister and more dangerous because of the involvement of outside powers and the availability of more destructive firepower at a time when the Sudan is beset with enormous problems of drought, desertification, agonising institutional disruption and a staggering international debt (most of which are compounded by the fact and requirements of the war).

These problems are crying for a determined national effort in order to find solutions. It is absolutely essential, therefore, to bring the civil war to an end as a first step towards economic and social health and recovery.

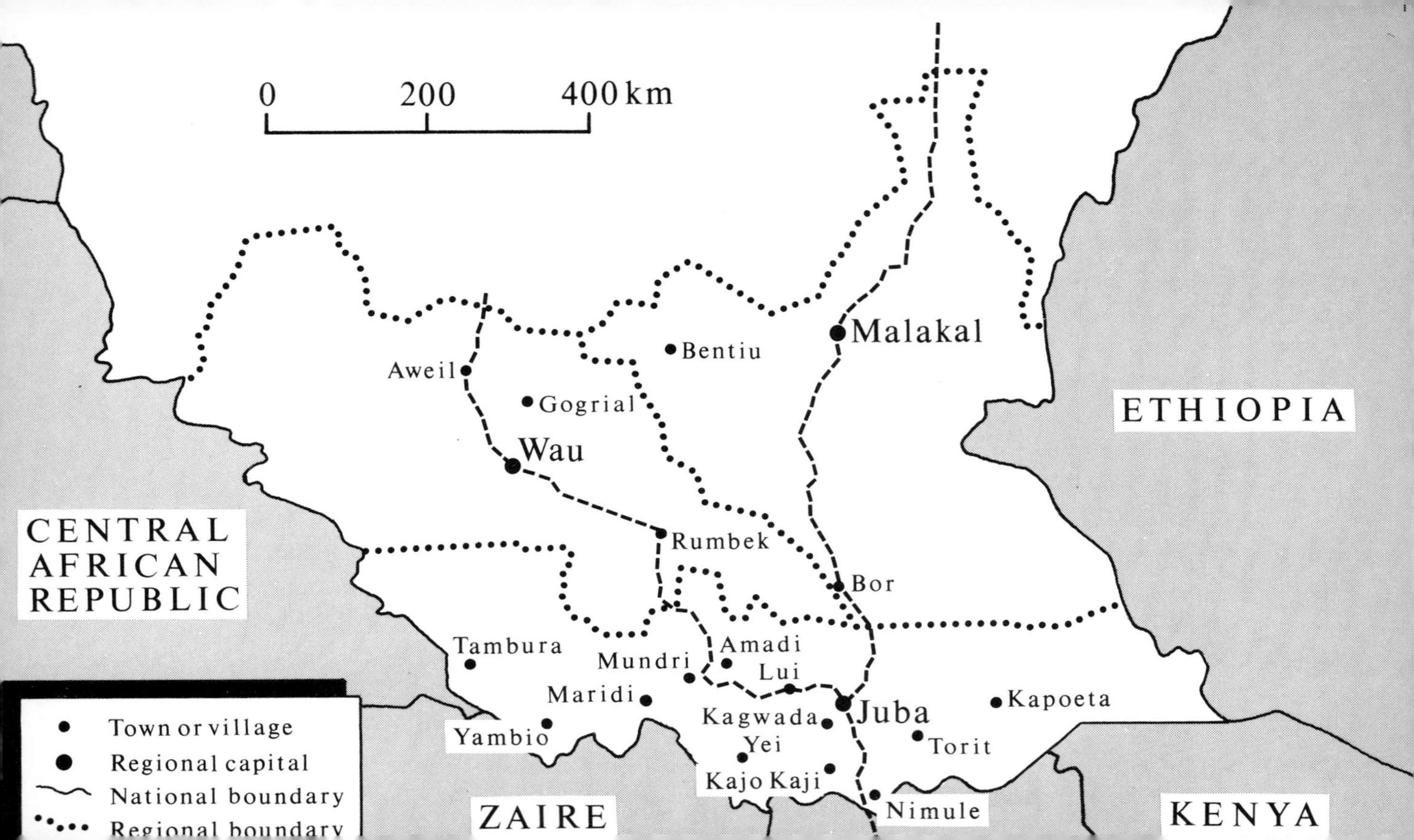
0
200
400 km
Malakal
Bentiu
Aweil
Gogrial
Wau
ETHIOPIA
CENTRAL
AFRICAN
REPUBLIC
Rumbek
Bor
Tambura
Amadi
Mundri
Lui
Maridi
Juba
Kapoeta
Kagwada
Yambio
Yei
Torit
Kajo Kaji
Nimule
ZAIRE
KENYA
Town or village
Regional capital
National boundary

AID AT A STANDSTILL

BEATRICE KHAMISA BAYA

Beatrice Khamisa Baya graduated from Khartoum University in 1985 with an Honours degree in political science. She has an MA in development studies from the University of Toronto and is currently studying for a PhD in political science at the same university. She specialises in development issues, with particular interest in aid and development, gender and grassroots politics in Africa.

All development projects in southern Sudan are virtually at a halt. That is the effect of the war.

It spells the death of hopes of closing the poverty gap between north and south Sudan: the south is estimated to have a per capita income of US$150 a year, compared with US$320 for the entire country. If anything, this disparity will grow wider.

Yet, southern Sudan is strong in natural resources and full of development opportunities — if only appropriate development strategies can be formulated in conditions of peace.

The region is, overwhelmingly, virgin territory. The area under cultivation is estimated at only 12%. It has immense potential for agriculture with favourable soils and rainfall. It also has a substantial forest area of around 155,000 square kilometres (96,900 square miles).

The economy is based on subsistence and semi-subsistence agriculture, with little manufacturing or organised commerce. Imports and exports are limited. The main occupation is agriculture and 91% of the people are rural.

Smallholders with no registered land, lacking capital and using

Robert Purnell

family labour to cultivate a small piece of land around the homestead, make up 98% of the farmers. Most use simple hand tools in clearing and cultivating land. Manual labour is virtually the sole source of farm power: only 2% of agricultural production uses animal and mechanical power. Except for government and donor aid projects, there is virtually no largescale farming.

The major crops are dura (a variety of sorghum), maize, millet, groundnuts, sesame and cassava. The region exports small quantities of crops, mainly cotton, tea, coffee and tobacco.

Major obstacles to development include shortage of investment funds for agriculture, limited use of fertiliser, lack of improved varieties of seed, and poor methods of cultivation. These are further restricted by inadequate agricultural training and extension services, the poor transport network — particularly in the rural areas — the lack of efficient urban and rural markets, as well as smallholder agricultural credit and the isolation of southern Sudan itself.

Clearly, therefore, the lack of a basic and viable infrastructure is the major single constraint to development.

Not only is the region heavily dependent on subsistence agriculture but it actually has to import food. One government after the other has aimed at raising rural incomes by increasing productivity, especially in agriculture, but without success. The top official priority remains the development of the traditional agricultural sector.

The widespread poverty means that southern Sudan can raise only limited money through taxes; in addition, the amount allocated to it from the national treasury is small relative to its size and relative to the regional governments in the north. So the south has had to rely heavily on external capital to finance its development projects.

This capital usually comes in the form of foreign aid. Due to the extensive destruction during the 1955 – 1972 civil war, aid programmes for the region are geared towards both development and rehabilitation. Thus a large part of aid comes as grants.

Help through international bodies — multilateral assistance —is the most important source of finance for development. The bulk of this is provided by United Nations agencies, with support from others such as the European Economic Community (EEC) and the World Health Organization (WHO).

The second most important source of aid is from foreign governments and agencies direct to the Sudan Government. At the time of writing, there are 25 of these bilateral development donors. Until 1985, the United States was providing an average 42% of Sudan's total official development assistance. Sudan was third on the list of "most favoured" US nations in terms of aid, after Israel and Egypt. In 1988, Sudan has dropped to sixth place, behind El Salvador, the Philippines and Pakistan, with the United States accounting for 32% of its aid.

Additional help comes from voluntary aid bodies. Examples of non-profit, non-governmental organisations (NGOs) are Norwegian Church Aid, which is involved in rural and water development, health dispensaries, schools and infrastructure rehabilitation; the Lutheran World Service, which runs rural development projects plus education and primary health care programmes; and the Sudan Council of Churches which is involved in integrated rural development and women's work, well-drilling, ox-training and providing agricultural tools and horticultural seeds on credit.

In 1979 – 1980, total donor aid to the southern Sudan was £S27 million (US$6.75 million). The NGOs contributed about a fifth of this.

Although most of the aid from foreign governments and international bodies is allocated to agriculture, about half of this has been for large capital intensive schemes — with emphasis on planning, and hence future benefits. NGOs, on the other hand, go for projects which can offer greater immediate benefit to farm families.

Foreign aid runs at more than three times the amount which southern Sudan itself can muster for development from its domestic resources. This raises the question whether continuous aid for development — especially when it appears to be substituting for, rather than supplementing, domestic resources — is a wise and viable strategy.

What has been the impact of the war on development efforts in southern Sudan? Obviously, the war raises serious questions not only for the present but for the future too.

The impact of the war can be gauged by looking at some of the development projects in the south — at a canal scheme and an oil pipeline under the direction of the central government; and, as development projects are donor-financed, at two USAID projects in agriculture and transport.

Two projects halted

Since 1984, the Sudan People's Liberation Army (SPLA) has successfully forced a halt to work on the two biggest development projects in southern Sudan. The first is the 320 kilometre (200 mile) Jonglei Canal Scheme, initiated in 1978. The canal is a joint venture between the Sudanese and Egyptian governments. It is intended to increase the flow of water in the White Nile to the north by diverting 20 million cubic metres of water daily from the Sudd marshlands, that is, shortening the river from south to north.

The scheme aims to conserve more than 10% of the 33,000 million cubic metres of water lost annually through evaporation.

Katri Burri/Panos Pictures

This 2,000 tonne excavator was purchased for the Jonglei Canal Scheme, and was at that time the biggest machine in the world. It was shipped from Pakistan to Port Sudan, then by rail to Khartoum and by river to Malakal, where it was reassembled. It has reportedly now been dismantled and turned into cooking pots, tools and spears.

This would be used to irrigate an extra 3 to 4 million feddans (3.1 to 4.2 million acres) of land in central Sudan and a similar area in Egypt.

The scheme is also purportedly aimed at aiding the south by upgrading 1.5 million hectares (3.7 million acres) of agricultural land and opening up large parts of it to "modern" agriculture.

But this last objective is rather dubious. There is no shortage of cultivable land in the region; on the contrary, estimates put the total area of arable land under cultivation at only 12% (and some estimates are even lower). Aiding southern Sudan should mean assisting in the full harnessing of the huge existing potential, rather than adding what would at this stage amount to superfluous agricultural land.

Not unexpectedly, therefore, many southerners have viewed the Jonglei project as exploitative and have opposed it from the start. There were student riots in the region over the issue and the project was one of the SPLA's first principal targets. Digging the canal was suspended in 1983 when it was more than two-thirds finished, after SPLA attacks on construction workers.

With no end to the civil war in sight, and given the severe deterioration of the security situation in the south, there are no prospects that the canal scheme will be resumed in the near future.

The second project is the construction of an oil pipeline from Bentiu in Bahr el Ghazal region, in which the US oil company Chevron has invested US$90 million. The pipeline was to have carried oil from the two fields of Heglig and Unity to Port Sudan for export.

The known petroleum deposits are in the south and west of Sudan and have a potential annual revenue of US$136 million. However, the bulk of the commercially viable deposits are in the south. The Unity field alone has confirmed flows of over 50,000 barrels per day (b/d).

Plans to construct a 25,000 b/d refinery at Kosti, just outside the southern region, at an estimated cost of US$900 million were shelved in September 1982. Instead, the central government opted for the construction of a 1,400 kilometre (875 mile) export pipeline between the Unity field and a new terminal to be built near Port Sudan, at an estimated cost of about US$960 million!

This move was preceded by a northern attempt to change regional boundaries so that Bentiu, where the pipeline was to start, fell in the north. This created uproar in the south. Again, it was not surprising that the pipeline became one of the SPLA's first major targets. Attacks on Chevron's oilfield operations caused the company to suspend work in February 1984. By mid-1984, it was obvious that the project could not continue.

In mid-1988 it was reported that up to 2,000 government soldiers were to be sent in to guard the oilfield, and that this was coupled with renewed official pressure on Chevron to resume operations.

Both the Jonglei Canal Scheme and development of the south's oil reserves were viewed as vital to Sudan's long-term economic recovery. The potential revenue expected from oil provided the central government's main hope of overcoming its chronic balance of payments problems: oil accounted for 21% of the total import bill in 1984/85.

The suspension of these projects has dashed the hopes of the central government. However, the impact is far from being so conclusive in the south. It appears that the halting of these major projects has not had any negative economic effects on the people and economies of the southern provinces.

Both projects were seen by many southerners as symbols of northern exploitation of the region with the south standing to gain very little, if anything. It was argued that the Jonglei Canal would create major ecological changes which would not only significantly affect wildlife, but would also severely upset the traditional livelihood of the local people.

At the same time it was felt that the central government had not provided any viable alternatives to counter expected disruption. In regard to oil, it was generally felt that the move to build a pipeline to Port Sudan rather than construct a refinery at Kosti was prompted by northern self-interest. It does appear that both projects are geared to the needs of northern (rather than southern) Sudan, and in the case of Jonglei, to Egypt too.

US aid projects

A brief look at US-financed development projects is instructive. USAID has provided substantial funds in the form of grants to the southern Sudan for a range of projects, including primary health care, agricultural research and manpower development.

The projects in the region which received the largest USAID funding are infrastructural and institutional, neither of which are directly beneficial to the small rural farmers, and which might even discriminate against them. For instance, agricultural research seems to be biased toward helping production by the wealthier farmers and the larger public schemes through irrigation, fertilisers, pesticides and cash-cropping.

Because the chosen projects do not offer much prospect for generating meaningful income and work for small farmers and the rural sector in general, their effect on underprivileged groups is not expected to be substantial. Most significantly, the projects do not quite reflect the major points in the region's development strategy. This is not to say that no development will occur; the argument rather is that it will largely bypass those who need it most.

Nonetheless, it is clear that the suspension of projects due to the war is a setback for both rehabilitation and development. This is generally true, in spite of the questionable benefits of some of the projects for the region's professed development strategy (based on agriculture), and the targets of that strategy (the rural sector and smallholder farmers).

USAID's two main projects are in agriculture and transport: the Southern Region Agricultural Development Project (SRAD) and the Southern Road Maintenance and Rehabilitation Project I (SORMAR I).

SRAD has nearly US$7 million available to it and comprises five major components "designed to promote increased agricultural production and incomes in the southern region of Sudan by relieving key constraints to private sector agricultural production, processing and marketing activities." The components are: agricultural marketing, manpower development and utilisation, budget and financial planning, and area development.

Project implementation began in 1984 with five experts. However, escalating insecurity in the south led to their withdrawal by mid-1985.

Certainly, SRAD had shortcomings which raised questions about its real beneficiaries. The most obvious lay in the scrapping of the feeder roads and extension components of the project, evidently the most important in reaching rural farmers. In the absence of these two, SRAD could no longer claim as its targets either the isolated rural farmers who make up 98% of the region's farmers or the rural people who are 91% of the total population. Despite this, there is no doubt that SRAD could have made some positive general contributions to the development of the south's agricultural base.

The SORMAR I agreement was concluded in August 1983. This project was to have been completed in September 1989 at an ultimate cost of US$18.24 million. It consists of road rehabilitation and maintenance in Equatoria and Bahr el Ghazal regions. Its purpose is to improve and preserve "critical access" on primary roads within the south by establishing an all-weather major trunk link for the 457 kilometres (285.5 miles) between the towns of Mundri, Rumbek and Wau so as to increase agricultural production and incomes in the region.

The project was gathering speed for take-off in 1985, but security conditions in the region have grounded it since then.

This project, too, gives rise to questions about its appropriateness. While motor traffic on roads in the former Upper Nile region is limited to the drier periods between January and May, there are several good gravelled roads in the provinces of Equatoria and Bahr el Ghazal. These are passable all the year round. However, some of the minor roads become impassable after rain, and there are no roads from farms.

In the absence of rural and feeder roads, it is doubtful to what extent isolated rural farmers would benefit from upgrading existing trunk roads to an all-weather standard.

On the other hand, the crucial role of transport in development cannot be overstated, especially in the mobility of resources, services

Stephen King/CAFOD

Producer groups and farming families were helped directly by NGOs.

and information. The mere improvement of existing roads could yield significant gains.

It should be noted that the disruption of communications has been a major SPLA strategy. A principal target is the destruction of transport links, especially with the north. The total result has been deterioration in the south's already erratic supplies, and the region's effective isolation.

Most roads are not safe due to the placing of landmines (for example, the Kapoeta and Torit roads which provide outlets to Kenya and Uganda), or due to SPLA attacks on vehicles (for example, on the Yei road). In late-1987, two trains coming from the north were destroyed and two besieged by the SPLA near the southern town of Aweil.

The impact of these disruptions on transportation, and hence on development activities, hardly needs to be stated. Because of this problem, only those projects within the town of Juba can be seen to be functioning.

Expulsion of NGOs

Meanwhile, various relief and rehabilitation organisations have been expelled by the central government, with negative implications for the south.

The government regularly accuses NGOs of conspiring with the SPLA. Such accusations have been levelled at ACROSS, World Vision and Lutheran World Service: in September 1987 they were given three weeks to leave the country. They were accused of engaging in activities "damaging to the security of the country" and of having "leapt beyond the boundaries of their prescribed missions". After appeal, their expulsions were confirmed in February 1988.

Compounding the difficulties of NGOs, their workers have often been caught in the crossfire of the war or been kidnapped. NGOs have also complained about the behaviour of some regional authorities. One incident occurred in Juba in February 1988, when the military commandeered or impounded 15 of the 20 trucks donated by the British Government through Oxfam for distributing relief food in Equatoria. The British Government strongly protested and all the trucks were returned, except for one which had apparently been destroyed by a grenade.

Given these circumstances, it is not surprising that hardly any NGOs still operate in the south. Essential services provided by NGOs in rural areas, such as primary health care, digging and maintaining wells and boreholes for clean drinking water, and extension support activities, have stopped.

As NGO projects typically had greater and direct benefit for isolated farming families than multilateral and bilateral aid projects, the impact of their suspension is bound to be more immediate and tangible, affecting great numbers of people. The problem of ensuring safe access and operating for NGOs in the south has been discussed between the central government and the SPLA through the mediation of the United Nations High Commissioner for Refugees (UNHCR).

Last, but not least, the war has caused incredible human suffering and has weakened the base of the region's human and capital resources. The latter is evident in the destruction of the physical infrastructure and the former in the undermining of the social infrastructure, whether health or education.

The ability of people to produce food has also been severely affected — a critical factor in a subsistence economy. When, in mid-1986, there was additionally drought, famine became a major problem in the south. United Nations' estimates put the number of people at risk of starvation at 2 million.

In the meantime, the deteriorating security conditions cannot but help ensure priority for development projects which focus on the urban elite. This is already happening. While rural primary health care, extension support and literacy work have been suspended, the more theoretical semi-urban and urban training projects have generally kept going.

Clearly, the war has had tragic effects on the activities of those trying to rehabilitate and develop the south, and has eroded the modest development gains of the region during the brief inter-war period between 1972 and 1983. In real terms, this implies a further widening of the development gap between the north and the south.

This disparity in both economic and socio-political terms has been the fundamental obstacle to the normalisation of north-south relations. It will continue so until the central government effectively addresses the country's imbalanced development and the linked structure of control.

THE CHALLENGE TO SURVIVE

THOMAS KEDINI

Thomas P. Kedini graduated from Khartoum University with a BSc in civil engineering. He went on to study in the United Kingdom and the United States, including a three-month development studies course at the Development Institute, University of California. He is currently Principal of the Lainya Vocational Training Institute.

A slight tap on the door diverted my attention from the letter I was struggling to draft.

"Come in," I said.

The door opened slowly until the full face of a nervous young man was visible.

"Oh! Luwala, it is you! Come in, come in please. Welcome please! We heard terrible things about your village!"

"Morning, Principal," my visitor saluted me as he grabbed the chair beside him and moved it as far as possible from me.

"Now, tell me what really happened?" I asked impatiently.

"Well, those people [the SPLA guerillas] came there and robbed people's properties; their clothes, their food and their goats. They drove the young men away to carry their loot. Some of them wanted to rape the women but some were good," my visitor said as he related the events of the raid on Kulipapa village a week before.

What about his plans now that he had graduated from the Lainya Vocational Training Institute, I asked him. And how had the community in Kulipapa village received him? Instead of answering, he produced a letter signed on behalf of the elders and committee members of Kulipapa Church.

"We are very grateful because our son has learnt the skill of carpentry," said the letter. "He will be able to construct the doors for our church and also furniture for the primary school. But now the situation in the village has become very bad. It is not safe for young men like Augustino Luwala. It is better for us old people because our time is over.

So we, the elders and members of the Kulipapa Church, have agreed that we send our boy back to school for more training and employment. He will not be useful to the community now and even to himself."

As I came to the end of the letter, I was utterly confused and was scratching my head furiously. I was embarrassed to discover that my visitor was noticing these reactions. I straightened myself up as if ready to say something, but there was nothing to be said. Finally I said, "So, you are back! And what are we going to do with you? We have no budget and besides, we are not supposed to keep trainees with us. They are to go to their communities which sent them."

My visitor was as quiet and still as a stone. An attractive idea came to my mind. So I passed the letter to the Academic Secretary to study the case and to submit his opinion to me.

The Academic Secretary checked with the head of the carpentry department who agreed to take Mr Luwala into his department as he was one of his brightest students. He would be paid from what he produced.

That was but the beginning. I had to travel to Juba for a meeting and upon my return I discovered four others had returned: they were also placed in various departments. That some trainees returned to the institute for employment was a painful thing for me to accept.

The above story illustrates the frustration of one of the main aims of Lainya Vocational Training Institute. Right from its inception the philosophy has been to encourage the promotion of self-reliance and self-sufficiency in the rural communities and in the refugee camps. This has been through training a few of the youth in basic rural and industrial skills of agriculture, horticulture, carpentry and joinery, building and masonry, blacksmithing, and appropriate technology and home economics and handicrafts.

Towards the end of the course, the trainees are exposed to some bookkeeping and management to equip them for organising their small individual and group enterprises in their various communities. Upon graduation, the institute provides basic tools to encourage them to return directly to their communities, rather than wandering about in search of employment elsewhere. The community provides living accommodation, a plot of land and some capital for purchase of initial raw materials, for example, timber for carpentry students.

This philosophy took off fairly well and carpentry groups were seen in refugee camps. Graduates also established workshops in Kajokaji, Mundri, Maridi and as far as Yambio. There were groups in church parishes in the towns of Yei and Juba.

But the most spectacular has been the women carpentry group formed by three girls we trained in the institute. It results from the efforts of the Women Self-Help project in Yei. Many inquisitive people come to watch the girls work. The girls work well enough to convince each visitor not to leave without buying a wooden carved tray, a plate or even a set of chairs.

Disaster fell on our efforts in the rural areas and refugee camps when the SPLA operations and raids increased in the countryside. The camps were eventually shut down by the United Nations High Commissioner for Refugees (UNHCR) authorities and the refugees either repatriated back home to Uganda or re-allocated in other camps near the towns.

In local villages such as Rokon, Kulipapa and Kagwada the graduates fled to Juba, and others sought refuge in the institute itself, in the same way as Augustino Luwala.

The government in southern Sudan had a total of five technical secondary and vocational schools in the mid-1970s. Several experienced financial and staffing difficulties and only two survived until 1985. These were the May Vocational Training Centre in Wau and Torit Technical Secondary School. They were forcefully shut down by the shelling and subsequent surrounding of Wau and Torit towns during the SPLA offensive in 1985.

With the death of these two institutions, there us only was in

Women students practicing ox-ploughing at Lainya. But the oxen were slaughtered and eaten by SPLA troops when they attacked the institute in October 1986.

Lainya Vocational Training Institute, with a little moral support from the Multipurpose Training Centre in Juba— though its objectives are not quite identical to ours.

We at Lainya owe our survival, not so much to the fact that we are in a more secure place, but to our strong financial backing coupled with the determination and dedication of our staff. When Lainya was opened five years ago it benefited from the refugee funds operated by the then Southern Sudan Refugee Assistance Project (SSRAP).

When the project ended in 1985, our funding continued through other organisations. The SSRAP director had filed applications to the Ford Foundation and others for direct funding for the Lainya programme. The results were successful, hence we cruised on as if nothing had happened.

However, starting mid-1986, security in and around Lainya began to be worrying. The town of Lainya was threatened by SPLA guerillas. We had to flee with the students to Yei but nothing serious happened.

Eventually, Lainya was attacked in October that year and a greater part of the town, including the institute's premises, fell into the hands of the SPLA for half a day. The institute sustained considerable losses and damage to property and equipment. Two of our trained ploughing oxen were slaughtered.

However, apart from that, nothing to prohibit our training was experienced and so, after a month's absence, both staff and students voted to return to the institute and continue with business.

In mid-1987, the pressure from the SPLA was again increasing and this time we began to experience problems from the staff and students. Complaints of low pay, lack of incentives and inadequate care were being regularly heard from the staff. The students were becoming impatient with their food and conditions.

We felt it was time to move out of Lainya. On 2 October we moved the students and staff to Yei town and that is where the school is at the moment.

The greatest harm caused by this moving up and down is the failure to consolidate our self-reliance efforts. The school garden was never well attended, the sawmill was not working, the carpentry workshop never progressed, the guest house furniture was looted, and so on.

Our dream was to establish income-generating activities which would support us in the future. With all this instability we had to continue to depend solely on funds from abroad. As the road ahead still looks dark it is difficult to visualise what could happen five to ten years from now when the donors finally release us to our fate.

As the news of insecurity and instability began to reach our donors, some began to be sceptical about supporting a project whose activities they might not have the slightest chance of monitoring. For example, Catholic Relief Services had no appetite for funding beyond the two-year commitment ending in 1987. PECUSA did not even respond to our 1987 budget proposal. Band Aid and the Ford Foundation responded, but only to about half the 1987 budget.

If, in 1987, we were able to raise only half the budget, what about 1988 and the years ahead?

We had also started to face considerable difficulties in the delivery of our goods and materials. Due to the war in Uganda, and complicated by our own conditions in Sudan, goods travelling from Kenya had to be escorted by the army. Materials took ages to reach some of our programmes.

Whenever we had delays, work slowed and redundancies were created. We would then be obliged to streamline the labour force and that is when trouble came. Some individuals would threaten to beat up the foreman and "whoever may be concerned" for being non-co-operative and not being sensitive to the development needs of the surrounding community.

Survival for an institution, especially in the midst of the circumstances described above, is not much different from that of the human being; only the nature and proportions might be different. With the closing of the government training institutions it becomes more difficult to believe that one is alive while everybody else around you lies dead. The temptation is to pull the trigger and join the rest in the everlasting peace. But it may be wiser to face the challenge of staying alive.

We fear that, with the complete blackout of skills' training in southern Sudan, the problem will not only be lack of artisans but a society of survivors with too many mouths and too few hands to feed them. As Lainya continues to turn out a modest number of skilled personnel year after year, they will (if they survive) assist in development even just to care for their own mouths (self-reliance).

That is our vision at Lainya. We feel that, at this time, when things appear so gloomy, so hopeless, so frustrating and so depressing, we must not shy away from the challenge of survival now and for the future.

CUT OFF FROM HEALTH CARE

OLIVER M. DUKU

Dr Oliver Meru Duku graduated from Khartoum University in 1963 with a degree in medical science. He then spent five years in West Germany where he obtained degrees in clinical chemistry and microbiology. In 1974, Dr Duku went to Juba to join the Regional Ministry of Health. From 1985-1988, he worked as project manager with the WHO/UNICEF joint nutrition support programme, based in Juba. In June 1988, he was appointed project leader for the AMREF/WHO rural health support project.

Five months before the flags of Britain and Egypt came down from the palace poles in Khartoum, to be replaced by the flag of the newly independent Sudan, southern Sudanese elements in the Sudan Defence Force mutinied at Torit in Equatoria province. This ushered in the first civil war which ravaged southern Sudan, especially Equatoria and Upper Nile provinces, for 17 years.

Only after the death of thousands of people, and the destruction of many health and educational facilities, did the combatants sit down in Addis Ababa in 1972 to sign an agreement to end the war and create a semi-autonomous region in southern Sudan.

Before independence, medical services were part of the colonial administration. The emphasis was on curative health care provided in hospitals and rural dispensaries. In southern Sudan there were 23 hospitals and about 50 rural dispensaries. One rural hospital in Lui, Equatoria province, was run by the Church Missionary Society. Attached to this was a centre for treating leprosy, and several rural health units.

The government took these over after independence, but they were destroyed during the war.

These district and rural hospitals and dispensaries were well equipped and regularly received with medical supplies. They were run by expatriate British, Egyptian and Syrian doctors, with a few northern Sudanese doctors.

The local southern Sudanese provided the nursing and other auxiliary medical staff. They also staffed the rural dispensaries under supervision of expatriate and northern Sudanese district medical inspectors and this continued after independence. Training of the local staff — medical assistants, laboratory assistants, and public health assistants such as sanitary overseers — was done at the Juba Training Centre. Nurses were trained on the job in provincial and district hospitals.

After independence, most of the expatriate doctors were replaced by Sudanese: medical officers came to southern Sudan from the north. The first southern Sudanese doctor graduated from Khartoum University in 1962; the year before, two southern Sudanese doctors had qualified at Egyptian universities. But it was not until 1964 that any southern Sudanese doctor was posted to hospitals in the south.

With intensification of the war, especially from 1962 onwards, health institutions in the rural areas of southern Sudan rapidly deteriorated. Rural dispensaries and some rural hospitals were destroyed and equipment looted. Staff abandoned these facilities and escaped into the bush or into the neighbouring countries as refugees, or migrated into the main towns in the south.

Large numbers transferred

A large number — including the writer — were transferred to the northern Sudan for fear that they might escape into the bush and join the rebels. By the end of the civil war in 1972, only 18 of the 23 hospitals were still functioning, although very poorly equipped and poorly supplied.

The southern regional government set up in 1973 embarked on the resettlement of people displaced by the fighting. There was a rush of aid from friendly governments and international and non-governmental voluntary organisations, joining hands with the Sudan government to restore hospitals and dispensaries.

The United Nations High Commissioner for Refugees (UNHCR) provided equipment and 27 ambulances and nine lorries, as well as funds and materials for rebuilding 75 dispensaries. The World Health Organization (WHO) and the United Nations Children's Fund (UNICEF) provided equipment. The Sudan Council of Churches rebuilt three rural hospitals. German Caritas reconstructed rural hospitals in western Equatoria. Lutheran World Service rebuilt a number of rural health facilities in Upper Nile province.

Thus, between 1974 and 1983, there was rapid development in the health field, with help from many governments and NGOs, ranging from the Netherlands, Norway and Britain to Kuwait.

Figure 1 (over the page) illustrates the results of this combined effort: 25 hospitals, 6 rural health centres, 80 dispensaries and 189 dressing stations were put into operation, even though many still needed work done.

In 1975, the government of the then Democratic Republic of the Sudan, with WHO help, investigated health in preparation for the National Six Year Socio-Economic Development Plan.

The National Health Programme which came out of this identified eight priority areas; of these, primary health care was given top billing. A population census in 1973 had shown that over 85% of the then 3 million people of the south Sudan lived in rural areas which were least provided with health services. Hence, the importance of starting a primary health care programme.

Thus, with strong backing from NGOs, by 1983 the government had running no less than 34 hospitals, 16 health centres, 176 dispensaries and 746 primary health care units.

Despite this effort, most of the hospitals were still in a bad state of repair. Essential equipment such as hospital beds, X- ray and operating equipment were poorly maintained.

Two influential events

Then, in 1983, two important events seriously affected the situation in southern Sudan.

First, the sudden break-up of the southern region into three separate regions, popularly known as *Kokora* or Redivision, required creation of three separate health administration units, one for each region.

Unfortunately, most of the senior health officials in the undivided southern Sudan administration were natives of Equatoria. Only the Director of Primary Health Care and his deputy came from Bahr el Ghazal. There was no-one from Upper Nile.

Hence, while management in the health department in Equatoria was hardly affected by the redivision, both Bahr el Ghazal and Upper Nile experienced severe shortages. This affected proper

Figure 1

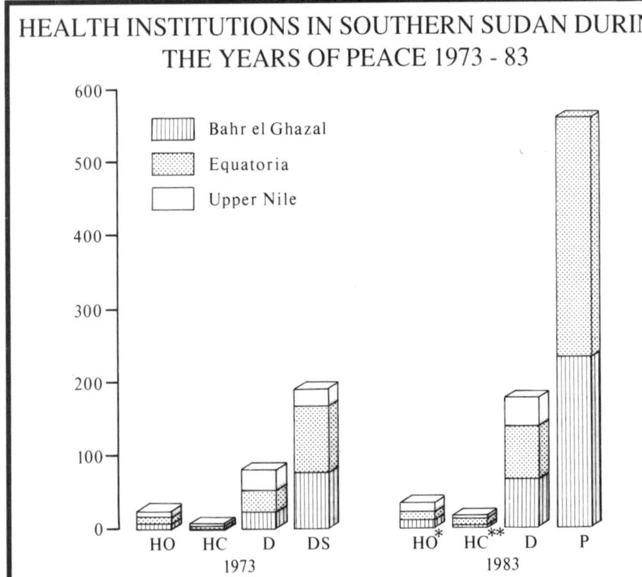

HO=hospitals (*includes hospitals still under construction but functioning as dispensaries to render services)
HC=Health centres, urban and rural
(Rural health centres still under construction but functioning as dispensaries or health units).**
D=Rural dispensaries
DS=Rural dressing stations
P=Primary health care units which include remodelled dressing stations.

Wendy Wallace

A primary health care worker in Bahr el Ghazal receiving a small supply of medicines. But this was in 1984: today, the supplies are no longer getting through.

planning and control of health services in the two regions.

Second, the fresh outbreak of hostilities in 1983 progressively affected more and more areas of Upper Nile and Bahr el Ghazal, and eventually most parts of Equatoria as well.

In 1988 (see Figure 2, over) only four provincial hospitals, 11 district and one rural hospital and three rural health centres are functioning. Except for Juba Teaching Hospital (maintained by German Technical Assistance, GTZ), el Sabah Children's Hospital

HEALTH INSTITUTIONS FUNCTIONING IN SOUTHERN SUDAN 1973,1983 AND 1988

Figure 2
HOSPITALS

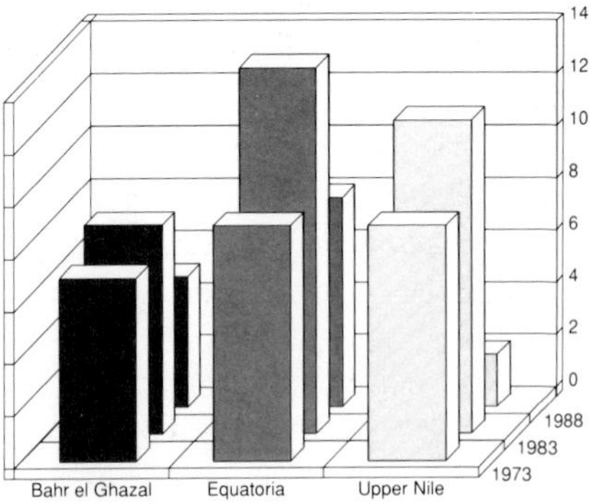

14
12
10
8
6
4
2
0
1988
1983
1973
Bahr el Ghazal
Equatoria
Upper Nile

Figure 3
DISPENSARIES

80
70
60
50
40
30
20
10
0
1988
1983
1973
Bahr el Ghazal
Equatoria
Upper Nile

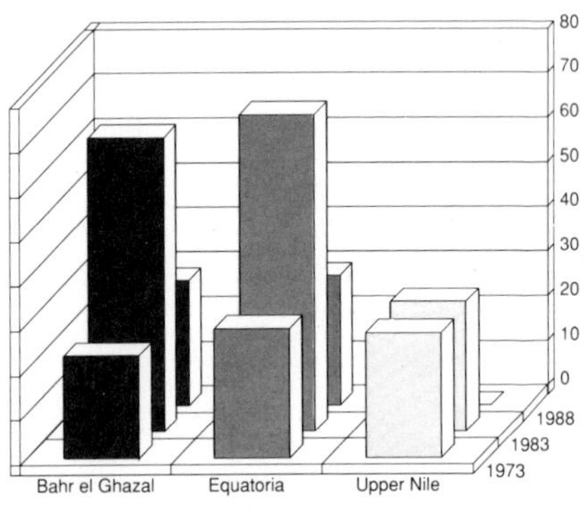

Figure 4
PRIMARY HEALTH CARE UNITS

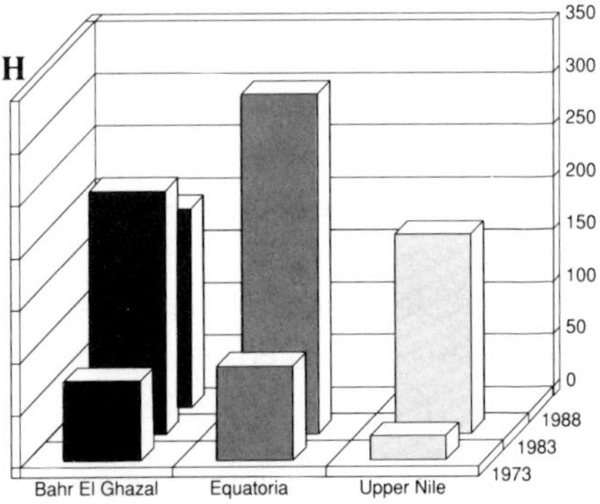

350
300
250
200
150
100
50
0
1988
1983
1973
Bahr El Ghazal
Equatoria
Upper Nile

in Juba (run by the Islamic Dawa Organisation), and Wau Regional Hospital (maintained by Sudan Aid), all hospitals and health centres are in a poor state.

Due to transport problems and lack of money, equipment is in short supply. Essential drugs are lacking in all hospitals and health centres. Even when medical supplies are available in the country they can be stranded in the central medical stores in Khartoum.

And although air transport to Juba from Khartoum and abroad might be available, depending on the security situation, the costs are prohibitive — such as, on cargo flights from Khartoum, £S4 (US$1) per kilogram.

UNICEF and WHO occasionally bring some medical supplies into Juba and so do NGOs. But these cannot easily be distributed in the surrounding districts or in the other two regions because of the insecurity of land transport and the non-existence of other means of transport.

The most disruptive effect of the present war is seen in the rural areas. This is illustrated in the tables opposite.

This year, hardly any rural health facility is functioning in southern Sudan. Only in western Equatoria province, where the SPLA have not yet established themselves, are rural health centres and a rural hospital still functioning.

The staffing situation in health is pathetic. Except for Juba Teaching Hospital and el Sabah Children's Hospital, where the teaching staff of the College of Medicine, Juba University, are helping, most functioning hospitals have no civilian doctor.

In Equatoria, only Yei and Yambio hospitals have doctors — one Sudanese each. Maridi hospital has one expatriate doctor. A few expatriate volunteer doctors are working in primary health care and specialised programmes, such as sleeping sickness control, in western Equatoria province. Wau and Malakal are run by single civilian doctors.

Basic health services, where they exist, are maintained only by medical assistants and nurses.

Doctors displaced

As with the people of the rural areas, the war has displaced most doctors and paramedical staff to urban centres, chiefly Juba and Khartoum.

It is only in these urban centres that the medical personnel can get their monthly salaries. In districts of Equatoria where branches of the Unity Bank are still open, as in Yei and Yambio, salaries are remitted regularly from Juba; other staff go for months without pay.

Another effect of the shortages of medicines and other medical supplies has been the increasing number of patients referred to Khartoum or Nairobi for medical care. Lack of specialist doctors and poor laboratory and X-ray diagnostic facilities also contribute to the mass referrals of patients, which are limited only by financial constraints and transport difficulties.

Primary health care is essentially community-based. The key components are health education, monitoring mother and child health growth, and immunisation. These are preventive and promotive health care elements. How has the war affected them?

In southern Sudan, primary health care is rural-based. Figures 2–4 show that the period of peace following the Addis Ababa agreement was marked by major strides in extending health care. International and non-governmental organisations played a key role in bringing about this progress.

Figure 4 also reveals the devastating effect of the war, which broke out in 1983, on the primary health care programme.

UNICEF and WHO had contributed a great deal, especially towards childhood immunisation and control of diarrhoeal diseases in children. Other NGOs immunised children against TB, measles, diptheria, whooping cough and poliomyelitis, and supplied food for malnourished children.

These programmes are, however, drastically reduced in scope and coverage by the war. Immunisation, growth monitoring and nutrition rehabilitation programmes are now limited to Juba, Yei, Yambio, Maridi and Tambura in Equatoria, and Wau town in Bahr el Ghazal.

On the positive side, an accelerated immunisation programme launched in Juba in April 1987 was very successful: more than 75% of children under one year of age were given full immunisation

Wendy Wallace

against the six childhood immunisable diseases. It is hoped that the goal of immunisation of 90% of children under one year by 1990 will be realised in Juba and in the camps for displaced persons around the town.

Unfortunately, however, this success story cannot be repeated in the rest of the south because of the war.

Growth monitoring and nutrition rehabilitation are also limited to these same areas.

Malnutrition, especially among children under 12, is prevalent. Two surveys carried out in Juba in 1986 and 1987 revealed that 9.8% of children under one year suffered from severe malnutrition — that is, weight for height was less than 60%. This is likely to grow worse as a result of the food shortages and displacement of the rural food-producing population into urban areas as a result of SPLA activities.

More than 80,000 people have been displaced into Juba from rural areas of Equatoria. Similar moves have occurred into the towns of Yei, Wau and Malakal.

SPLA actions continue to extend to more areas of south Sudan, thus disrupting agricultural work in the villages. The food supply situation in Juba and other main towns continues to deteriorate.

The present unacceptably high infant mortality rate — 180 per 1,000 live births — is certain to worsen as a consequence of the war and the hunger resulting from the disruption of agricultural activities in the food-producing areas.

The war has also reduced the already poor data collection essential for planning health programmes and monitoring changes in health status, especially of vulnerable groups.

The two sides in the war continue to escalate their weapon supplies and there seems to be no inclination to talk peace on either side. We are therefore likely to see further deterioration in the health and nutritional status of the 6 million people of southern Sudan.

THE CIVILIANS SUFFER MOST

COLE P. DODGE AND SIDDIQ ABDEL RAHMAN IBRAHIM

Cole P. Dodge graduated from the universities of California and Washington, USA with Masters' degrees in social anthropology and public health. Since 1965, he has worked with the US Peace Corps, the American Friends Service Committee, and Oxfam. Cole Dodge joined UNICEF in 1980 and was appointed representative in Uganda in 1981. Since 1982, he has served as UNICEF representative in Sudan.

Siddiq Abdel Rahman Ibrahim obtained a degree in politics at Lancaster University in Britain and a Master's degree in national development and project planning at Bradford University, Britain. In January 1986, he joined UNICEF Sudan office in the emergency section, where he initiated a vagrant children/street kids project. He also administered logistics and supplies for famine-afflicted areas of the country. Since May 1987, he has been Assistant Information Officer for UNICEF Sudan.

The nature of war has changed in two respects in this century. First, weaponry has changed for the worse: guns, bombs and mines are now more lethal. Secondly, civil war has increased in underdeveloped countries of Asia, Africa and Latin America.

These changes have resulted in an alarming impact on the civilian population with civilian casualties increasing from 10% in the First World War to 50% by the Second World War, to over 80% in all subsequent wars.

Sudan is no exception. It is the civilians who suffer most in direct as well as indirect ways.

UNICEF — the United Nations Children's Fund — provides assistance to the Government of Sudan to improve the "life chances" of children, their mothers and families.

This is done through a concentration on specific programme activities such as Child Survival and Development and provision of clean water. To have the maximum impact, programmes covering water and integrated development for women are focused in the Red Sea province, Kordofan, Bahr el Ghazal and Equatoria regions.

Within the health sector, immunisation is a national programme which aims to immunise 90% of all new-born Sudanese children by the year 1990. It fits into the global objective of Universal Child Immunisation which has been adopted by African and Arab countries alike. Similarly, the Oral Rehydration Therapy programme, using a sugar and salt drink, is nationwide and aimed at control of diarrhoeal diseases.

Both are implemented through the Ministry of Health in Khartoum. Both have regional and district operations officers who carry out vaccination and distribution of oral rehydration salts in the rural areas in Sudan. Non-governmental organisations, religious institutions and voluntary organisations are often UNICEF's partners in carrying out these programmes.

The provision of drinkable water involves appropriate technology, which in the case of rural communities means

UNICEF

Handpump installed by UNICEF near Wau.

handpumps. However, to install a handpump, a borehole must first be drilled; this entails an expensive drilling rig, support trucks, casing, concrete aprons and the like, as well as back-up workshops, logistics capacity and technical assistance personnel. These are therefore geographically concentrated, in both northern and southern parts of the country.

Implementing programmes

The Sudanese Ministry of Finance and Economic Planning signs the overall Plan of Operation with UNICEF once every five years. The technical ministries are responsible, along with regional authorities, for implementation of programmes. UNICEF contributes a combination of supplies which account for about 70%, plus cash assistance 12% and technical assistance 12%.

For example, in the immunisation programme, UNICEF provides all vaccines for the six immunisable childhood diseases, as well as syringes, most of the vehicles and all of the cold-chain equipment to ensure that vaccines are kept at the correct low temperature right through until use in the village. With water programmes, UNICEF provides the drilling rigs, support trucks, pumps, casing, and reinforcing rods.

The ministry provides personnel, the administrative structure, the policy and the total implementation strategy for such programmes.

UNICEF officials help their government counterparts in such areas as surveillance and monitoring of diseases in health, and master drillers and mechanics in the water projects. All such UNICEF personnel provide support to the Sudanese civil servants who actually implement projects.

The performance of these programmes over the years is illustrated in the graphs and charts.

Figure 1 (over page) compares fully immunised children with DPT (Diptheria, Pertusis — whooping cough — Tetanus) in the six northern regions compared with similar immunisation in the southern regions. As can readily be seen, the south lags far behind with no prospect of catching up in 1988, nor as long as the war continues.

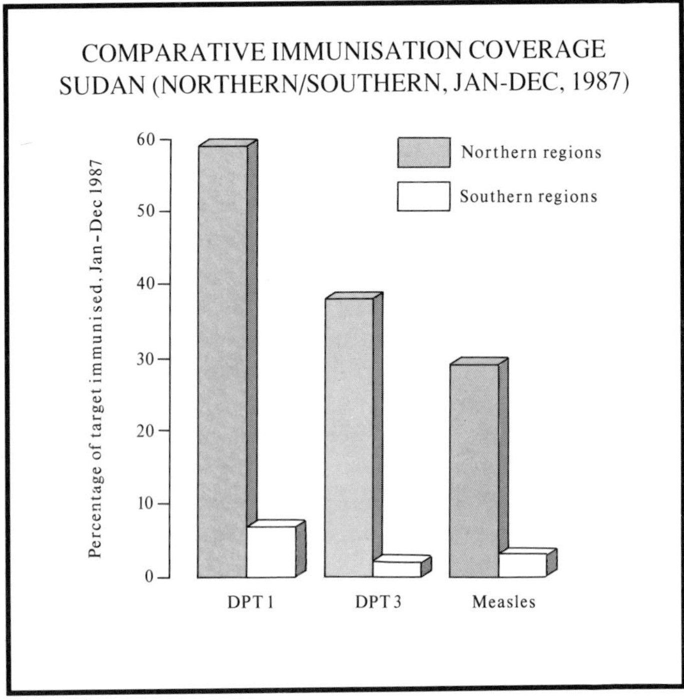

Figure 1

In the water supply sector, a comparison is made between the drilling programme in Bahr el Ghazal and Kordofan (see Figure 2 and Figure 3 on facing page). The impact of the war has led to a dramatic reduction in the drilling of new boreholes in the south, in contrast to the situation outside the region.

At the time of writing in 1988, the drilling programme has almost completely stopped in the south. But new levels of efficiency are being achieved in the north, resulting in a dramatic increase in clean water for thousands of rural northerners.

In the south, drilling has been concentrated in Wau town since 1985. No new handpumps have been developed outside of the city limits for the past three years. Yambio, on the other hand, is a relatively new programme, but despite stability in western Equatoria the programme has not gone forward due to disruption of supply lines.

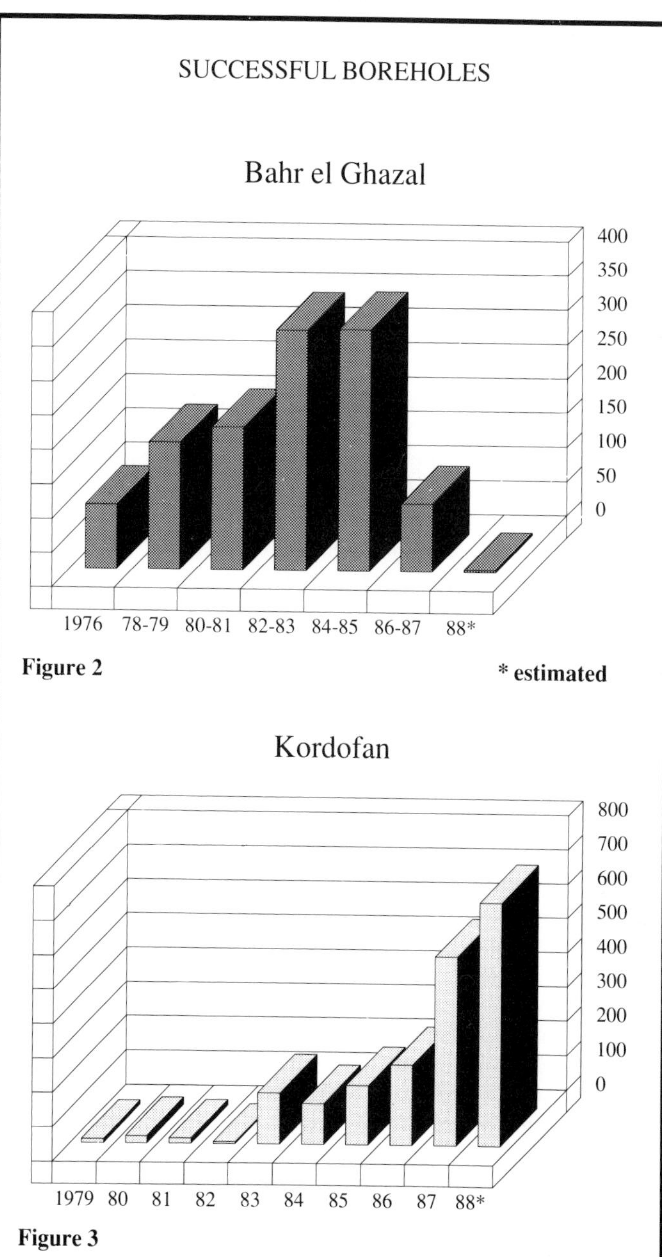

Figure 2

Figure 3

The problems facing implementation of UNICEF-assisted projects in southern Sudan include the following:

- Delivery of supplies: road transport from Kenya through Uganda to Juba has been severely disrupted. In March 1988 two trucks carrying fuel supplies for UNICEF programmes were attacked by rebels and burnt.
  The delivery of UNIMIX high energy food to Juba from Nairobi was delayed for four months in 1987 due to insecurity along the main route. Similarly, provision of medicines, vaccines, refrigerators and the like have been severely disrupted.
  All flights to Wau and Malakal by commercial carriers were stopped in August 1986 when the SPLA shot down a Sudan Airways passenger plane. This was followed by the shooting down of a SASCO charter aeroplane in May 1987. Thus even air transport to southern Sudan by expensive private charter companies has been impossible.
- The maintenance and repair of vehicles, equipment and refrigerators necessary to implement development schemes had become impossible by 1988 in southern Sudan. Spare parts necessary for the maintenance of equipment have not been delivered and old stocks are exhausted.
  Fuel is another problem. In Wau, for example, where we have drilling rigs and support trucks as well as government personnel capable of drilling boreholes, the price of fuel has gone to £S4,000 (US$1,000) per drum compared with £S150 (US$37.50) in the north. This is an impossibly high price to pay, so the project has come to a complete standstill despite the need for clean water.
  With thousands of displaced people seeking shelter, safety and food in the major southern towns, their health conditions are made worse by lack of safe drinking water. Similarly, the cold-chain has been difficult to maintain because of lack of batteries, fuel for generators and spare parts.
- Communications is another area of difficulty as the government security forces from time to time do not allow radio communication between locations in southern Sudan and Khartoum. This completely disrupts the tenuous links UNICEF has and discourages any type of work in the south.
  While it is true that Wau has been particularly affected by this disruption in communications it is also true, but to a lesser

extent, of the other two regional capitals and numerous smaller towns.

- Technical Assistance personnel cannot carry out normal work as the United Nations system has put southern Sudan on its highest level of evacuation. Only minimal essential personnel are allowed to remain in one region, Equatoria, and then only in two towns, Juba and Yei. There are no UN officials in Wau, Malakal, Yambio and other towns of the south.
- Salaries cannot be paid regularly to government civil servants as the communication system has been broken in Upper Nile and Bahr el Ghazal. This has been extremely disruptive to what little administrative capacity exists.

  Civil servants in Wau, for example, went on strike for four months in mid-1987, closing the hospital, schools and other social service facilities.
- Facilities such as hospitals and schools are not repaired and maintained and therefore fall into disrepair and eventual disuse. This makes it difficult to implement even emergency programmes.

  For example, when officials of the International Committee of the Red Cross (ICRC) went to Wau in June 1988 they found the hospital abandoned and empty; even basic furniture was missing.
- There are ethnic differences in many locations in the south. It is not only a war between army and SPLA but southern militia have also been armed to assist the army in defending civilian populations. Deep animosities between some southern ethnic groups are aggravated by too many guns.

  For example, in June 1987, an immunisation team went into a neighbourhood of Wau town and one of them was killed by the people because he was from a rival tribal group.

Despite the commitment ...

While the Ministry of Health and the National Water Corporation are fully committed to implementing programmes in southern Sudan, the graphs dramatically illustrate the decline in UNICEF programme achievements.

Because UNICEF has a mandate to reach children in areas of armed conflict we probably try harder than other international agencies to provide assistance to civilians in southern Sudan. As such, the military authorities have allowed UNICEF aircraft to fly

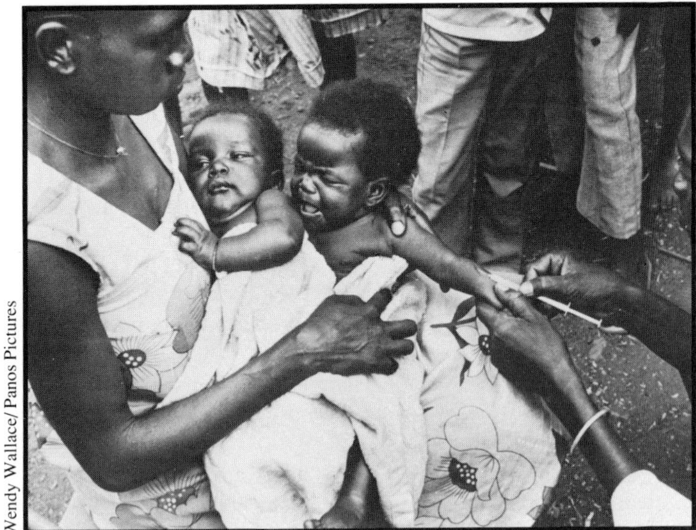

Wendy Wallace/ Panos Pictures

Vaccination clinic in southern Sudan run with UNICEF support.

Ministry of Health vaccines, oral rehydration salts and maternal child health medicines to four locations in the south in 1988.

This accounts for what limited immunisation services there are in Wau and Malakal. On the other hand, Juba and Yei are supplied by commercial carriers and UNICEF aircraft from the Ministry of Health in Khartoum.

UNICEF and Médecins Sans Frontières-Holland fielded an emergency medical team to work at the regional hospital in Wau, under agreement from the Khartoum Relief and Rehabilitation Commission and the Bahr el Ghazal regional authorities. Two Dutch doctors provided medical care and nutritional feeding in Wau hospital from March 1987 to January 1988.

Only critically-ill children were admitted to the small paediatric department: over half died. Similarly, UNIMIX high energy food was in very short supply but nonetheless we managed to run a nutrition rehabilitation centre for severely malnourished children: 20% of these children died.

By January 1988, the team was evacuated as the security situation was untenable in Wau.

EDUCATION: TOTAL COLLAPSE

PATRICIO ABIBO FULLY

Patricio Abibo Fully graduated with a degree in statistics. He is currently senior inspector of educational statistics and plánning with the Department of Educational Planning and Development Administration in the Directorate of Education and Guidance, Equatoria Region.

Those familiar with southern Sudan associate it with isolation and remoteness; as such, the people are viewed as among the most backward of the poorest nation in the African continent.

Any nation striving to improve the living standard of its people must increase their productive capacity. The one way to do this is through the provision of education.

Before the attainment of national independence, education in northern Sudan developed quite differently from that in southern Sudan in both form and content so that barely any similarity existed in the formal educational systems in the two parts of the country. Northern Sudan, perhaps due to its proximity to the Mediterranean and the Arab world, had the first educational establishments; in the south, education developed much later, and even then there was lack of interest in it.

After independence in 1956, the government embarked on education, prompted by the immediate need for trained indigenous manpower to fill the vacuum left by the departing British and Egyptians.

Nationally, pupil enrolment in primary education, for instance, increased from about 150,000 in 1956 to over 1,200,000 by 1977, and reached 1,653,491 by the 1984/85 school year. Between 1956 and 1977, intermediate level enrolment increased from barely 10,000 to 341,283. The number of senior secondary pupils jumped from 5,000 to 150,000 between 1956 and 1983.

But progress in education in the south was quite different. The national statistics barely give any information about the south. Progress there was hampered greatly by the first civil strife, from 1955 to 1972, when the meagre educational facilities were virtually brought to a standstill.

According to reports, by the mid-1960s many educational establishments had been taken over by the army and were used as barracks. In fact, even up to today, the army has not handed back some of these facilities to the educational authorities. Especially in the rural areas, many people fled; schools were abandoned and all their furniture, equipment and materials were lost.

After the hostilities

After the end of hostilities, brought about by the Addis Ababa agreement in 1972, the semi-autonomous southern regional government re-organised education. Many Sudanese, particularly southerners, and even the outside world, had hopes for the south's social and economic development. In education, the progress was comparatively significant: many educational establishments, formerly closed, were rehabilitated, educational facilities were provided in many rural areas, and the number of southern Sudanese attending national universities and higher institutes increased.

The number of primary schools in the south increased from 327 in 1973/74 to 777 by 1982/83; intermediate schools increased from 40 to 115, and senior secondary schools went up from a mere three to 28. Pupil enrolment for first-level education rose from 18% to 29%. Technical education and teacher training also improved significantly.

The quest for education was so great among southerners that the growth in the number of schools, especially at the lower level, was uncontrollable. Each village wanted a school and if the government could not build one, local communities — that is, parents — built it. Officially, such schools are referred to as "self-help schools".

Kator secondary school in Juba: abandoned.

The local communities established these schools with the intention of eventually handing them over to the government. But most schools were not planned in regional development budgets, and it became impossible to extend financial assistance to them.

The unplanned development carried other problems: schools were often overcrowded, especially in the lower classes, and did not have even minimal requirements for effective teaching; teachers were in short supply, particularly at the primary level, and many were untrained. The problems grew to the extent that, by the mid-1970s, strikes were common, especially in boarding-schools, because of lack of facilities. The regional government was finding it increasingly difficult to pay teachers' salaries.

Despite all these and many other complications, southern parents were determined to secure the education of their children and educational progress persisted.

The curse of the south

But as if the south has a permanent curse, a similar situation to that of the 1950s and 1960s has commenced again. The present war has brought not only education but all other development activities in all of the rural south, where most southerners live, to a total stoppage. The south is again in a civil turmoil, but of an even greater nature. Schools have been abandoned, and the pupils and teachers have moved to the urban centres where security prevails.

The state of education can rightly be described as total collapse.

Wendy Wallace

The short-term and long-term consequences of this collapse will be grave, and the economic implications devastating. The very low standard of life in the south will continue for a long time to come.

Measuring the government effort

Systems adopted for measurement of educational performance are usually inadequate, due to lack of basic data, lack of equipment and manpower requirements. The lagging behind of the developing countries in science, research and technology, has rendered the task of measuring educational performance, and hence, discovering faults, very difficult.

The extent of the government's effort in providing education is usually measured, in south Sudan's Directorate of Education, by examining schools in regard to the type of support they receive. By 1980/81 the government fully supported 76.73% of total primary schools. The extent of education by local communities is also clearly evident in the number of government-aided, self-help and private schools.

In the present war, the deserted rural schools have lost even the meagre facilities which they had — and with a great possibility that the actual buildings will collapse. Even if peace emerges, the economy of the Sudan will not allow for rehabilitation of these schools, let alone the provision of educational facilities, for a long, long time.

Another means of measuring the financial input into education — a method adopted by the Department of Educational Planning in southern Sudan — is to examine schools in terms of the building materials used for construction. In the south, some schools are permanently built — that is, with iron roofs, bricks, cement, etc — while others are built of semi-permanent materials, such as grass roofs and brick walls. Others are built completely of local materials — grass roofs, mud walls, bamboo, etc. Finally, others have no buildings: they either function under trees or in the buildings of another school.

A recent educational report found that most schools in the south were built of semi-permanent and local materials or had no buildings; only 25% were permanently built. Because of this, most schools usually do not operate after heavy rain or when it is raining,

TABLE SHOWING OPTIMUM EFFICIENCY INDICATORS

Level	Teacher/ class	Pupil/ class
Primary	1.25	50
Intermediate	1.50	45
Academic (secondary)	1.60	40
Technical (secondary)	1.75	35
Institute (secondary)	1.75	20

Source Fully P.A., "Progress in Education Systems of Educational Indicators in south Sudan 1973/74 — 1985/86", Juba, 1987.

and some schools — even in Juba town — have walls which have fallen down.

Hence the low performance within the educational system: its ineffectiveness and inefficiency could partly be attributed to the poor facilities. Dishearteningly, the southern government will not, in the near future, be able to alter this. The little finance injected into the system is thus actually a waste.

The number of classes or classrooms available is an indication of space availability as well as educational opportunity. Officially, optimum pupil per class ratios have been determined for efficiency and effectiveness as far as Sudanese education is concerned.

The actual observations between 1975 and 1983 clearly indicate how inefficient and ineffective the educational provision in the south has been: at all levels the number of pupils has diverged from the optimum values. Classes were overwhelmingly crowded, even at senior secondary levels. For instance, by 1983, there was a pupil to class ratio of 60:1 at the teacher training institutes, instead of the official 20:1 shown in the table.

On the other hand, the teacher to class ratio shows that teachers have always been in short supply for primary educational levels, while there were more than enough for the intermediate and secondary levels. At the Institute of Education there were twice the number required. However, most of them are untrained.

The educational system is further rendered ineffective by lack of basic facilities: many schools do not have desks, blackboards, textbooks, laboratories or libraries — or even water. No school except Torit Technical and Juba Girls is supplied with electricity.

Confusion and bureaucracy

Currently, the region is not in a position to do a thing to provide better facilities. Underlying this is a general state of confusion and unawareness in regard to educational facilities. The educational directorates in the southern region have become so bureaucratic and unsystematic that a properly planned and co-ordinated strategy for advancement is totally lacking, training of teachers has greatly diminished, and teacher training is dependent on personal influence rather than on educational goals.

Even most of the vehicles designated for developmental purposes have reached their salvage point, and the few which remain operate within a limited area of the towns.

Coupled with the lack of funds — money usually does not come at all from Khartoum — the future of education in the south is highly uncertain.

Thor Ullerø/Norwegian Church Aid

The shortage of teachers is a critical handicap: in 1983, of the 13,256 primary school teachers required, only 4,783 were supplied, or 36%. Ascending further on the educational ladder, even fewer teachers are available: at the secondary level, a mere 3% of the teachers required were available by 1975, and despite the intervening years of peace, only 7% by 1983.

Thus the provision of educational facilities is far behind the demand of the southern population, and is much lower than national average standards. The present provision is barely adequate to satisfy 10% of the demand.

In addition, teachers in southern Sudan have perhaps suffered more than other professions. Many in the south, and indeed in the Sudan as a whole, have a low opinion of teachers; the status of teachers is seen in their poor pay. The rectification of such misguided opinions is not easy. The southerners must accord to the teachers their importance in society, or what is now being experienced is likely to have very expensive results for the region.

Another important indicator of the inefficiency of the educational system is seen in a recent study of the flow of students between grades. An average rate of 10% for pupils repeating a class applies to the primary level; at the next level, repetition decreases to about 2%, and is almost 0% at secondary level. In addition, most pupils drop out of schooling, particularly during the starting grades, before they have learnt how to write; barely 50% of intermediate pupils proceed to senior secondary level, and even less than 1% of secondary pupils proceed further with education although they actually complete their level.

No single explanation

There is no single explanation for these discrepancies. There are certainly factors — socio-political, economic and demographic — which require closer investigation to understand the root of these problems. However, what all these findings point to is that the provision of educational facilities has not contributed to improved educational performance in southern Sudan.

In addition, Sudanese education has become highly politicised and schools in both the north and south have become centres for

Wendy Wallace/Panos Pictures

Bringi Primary School in Bahr el Ghazal. The children sit on mud bricks and use them as desks.

political activities. Hence, closures of schools and universities have become frequent. In the south the role which schools play in politics approached its peak in the mid to late-1970s.

As far back as 1953, however, the declaration of the unification of the Sudanese educational system was seen by southerners as a move towards the Arabisation of southern Sudanese. The southerners, who want to retain African cultures and values, responded negatively to this declaration.

The problem of language remains acute. For the most part, the south still insists on the English language. At the national level, however, Arabic is recognised; so most southern students do not, or may not, gain acceptance to certain faculties in universities and other colleges because they are not qualified in Arabic.

Many southern educationists and intellectuals have recently initiated debates on the issue. They believe that the Sudanese educational system is biased, one-sided and unworkable in the south and that reform is necessary.

But there is widespread confusion and it is doubtful what system of education the Sudanese people wish to develop.

LOSS OF THE REVERED CATTLE

SAM GONDA AND WILLIAM MOGGA

Dr Samuel Gonda went into exile in Uganda as a result of the civil war. He returned to Sudan and gained a Bachelor of Veterinary Sciences degree at Khartoum University and joined the Department of Veterinary Sciences. In 1982-83 he obtained a Diploma in Farm Management at Glinerimistan Agricultural College in Victoria State, Australia. In 1987 he was seconded to ACCOMPLISH, in charge of the organisation's livestock projects in Equatoria region.

Dr William Mogga, while a refugee in Uganda, obtained a Bachelor of Veterinary Medicine degree at Makerere University. He returned to Sudan to work as a veterinary officer and in agricultural planning. In 1980-84 he studied at Reading University, Britain, and gained an M.Phil in Veterinary Epidemiology and Economics. Since 1987 he has been Director-General of Animal Resources and Fisheries in Equatoria region.

The majority of southern Sudan's 6 million people are subsistence farmers, most of whom rely on transhumant pastoralism — the seasonal moving of livestock for pasture. They supplement this by growing food — using poor-quality implements and low-yielding crop varieties.

They are poor even in a poor country: when their per capita income was last measured in 1976, it was between US$80 – 150, compared with the Sudan national figure for the same year of US$290.

Their way of life is determined by their geographical environ-

J Bennett/Oxfam

ment: southern Sudan is a large basin which slopes both gently northwards and from the east to the west. It is drained mainly by the Bahr el Jabel River, which unites with its tributaries at the great swampy area known as the Sudd to form the White Nile River. Average annual rainfall is between 700mm – 1,600mm.

Three ecological zones

The south supports both subsistence and pastoral livestock systems and is divided into three major ecological zones:

CENTRAL RAINLAND — a predominantly flat savanna grassland with scattered thorn trees covering the northern parts of the Upper Nile region. The soil is mostly heavy clay, poorly drained and difficult to till, with cracks appearing in the dry periods. Average annual rainfall is between 700 – 800mm per annum lasting for four to five months in a year.

FLOOD PLAINS — these extend over half of the south with extensive transhumant livestock areas. Its four different land types vary from highlands which are free from annual flooding through to the Sudd which is a permanently flooded swamp. It is these land types which determine the location of permanent settlements of the pastoralists as well as their transhumant husbandry methods.

EQUATORIA — which covers the southern flank of the south. Vegetation ranges from open savanna grassland, with varying density of trees and bushes, to dense forests. Rainfall is between 900mm – 1,600mm for six to nine months in a year. Crop agriculture is predominant; keeping livestock is restricted to areas free of tsetse-fly.

The people

The people of southern Sudan are negroid as opposed to the mixed Afro-Arabs of the northern Sudan. They fall into three ethnic groups;

NILOTICS: form the majority group and occupy the flood plains and part of the central rainland zones. They comprise the Dinka, Nuer, Shilluk and other small tribes. They form the bulk of the transhumant pastoralists, owning about 85% of southern Sudan's cattle.

NILO-HAMITES: are found in Equatoria and include the Toposa, Bari and Latuko linguistic groups. The Toposa and the Mundari (from the Bari group) practise transhumant pastoralism, owning

about 12% of the southern animal population. The rest are sedentary subsistence and mixed farmers.
WESTERN SUDANIC: comprise the Azande, Moru/Madi of Equatoria, and the Ferlit of Bahr el Ghazal. Subsistence farming is practised, but keeping livestock is constrained by tsetse-fly.

A form of insurance

Livestock are crucial in the socio-economic structure of the pastoralists, apart from providing their milk-based diet, and meat to a secondary extent. For survival in their marginal environment, the pastoralists keep large herds of cattle as a form of insurance against natural environmental and man-made hazards, like drought, floods, epidemic diseases, intertribal and civil wars.

Herd sizes vary from ten to several hundred. When there is drought resulting in grain shortage, cattle — as well as sheep and goats — are sold or exchanged for grain. Social and cultural interactions relating to marriages, rituals, settlement of disputes — where killing is involved — and status also entail possession and disposal of large numbers of cattle.

This tendency to retain large herds of cattle is a universal phenomenon in pastoralist Africa.

The livestock-producing areas of the flood plains supply local towns and are the main exporters of cattle to the meat-consuming areas of Juba, Yei, Maridi, Yambio, Tambura and Mundri. In 1972, average meat consumption was 15 kilograms (33 lbs) per person a year; by 1981, after nearly 10 years of peace, it had risen to 26 kilograms.

The contribution of cattle to the general cash economy of south Sudan was, and is, limited. In 1955/56, just before the outbreak of the first civil war, the contribution of livestock to Sudan's GNP was 23.6%. The most recently available statistic is for 1971/72, when it was just 15.2%.

But the south could contribute much to its own economy, and to the general development of the Sudan, should positive developmental strategy and peace be possible. Traditionally, there was movement of stock to northern markets from Aweil, Gogrial, Bentiu and Malakal, although the economic impact has not been properly gauged.

The last estimates of livestock numbers were made in 1980/81. If we disregard the present war and use the same parameters as that study, the animal population of southern Sudan should now stand as follows (with a confidence limit of about 60%):

ESTIMATED LIVESTOCK POPULATION AND PERCENTAGES IN SOUTHERN SUDAN BY REGIONS, 1988 (in thousands)

Region	Cattle No's	%	Sheep No's	%	Goats No's	%
Upper Nile	4,452.2	50.9	1,747.1	38.3	1,242.2	41.7
Bahr el Ghazal	3,030.9	34.7	1,503.0	33.0	1,348.0	45.3
Equatoria	1,257.5	14.4	1,309.6	28.7	386.7	13.0
Total	8,740.6		4,559.7		2,976.9	

It is widely acknowledged that the livestock population has shown a steady increase since the turn of the century and especially after the end of the first 17 years' civil war. This was attributed to the introduction of vaccines for cattle diseases.

During the years of peace

During the 11 years of relative peace after the 1972 peace accord, the then southern government established a modest infrastructure which enabled livestock development programmes to be pursued.

Despite the unequal distribution of national wealth and resources by the central government in Khartoum, the first regional government staggered on to provide pastoralists with essential veterinary machinery, drugs, vaccines and most importantly, qualified staff to promote production and raise standards.

There were 24 district offices staffed by district veterinary officers with bachelor of veterinary medicine degrees. The offices were modestly equipped with diagnostic facilities, cold-chain and logistics for mass cattle vaccination programmes. The six veterinary provincial headquarters were staffed by senior veterinary officers. The headquarters in Juba was adequately staffed and was able to supervise the field services. But there was much to be desired in the buildings, veterinary clinics and logistics away from the towns in the producing areas where veterinary stockmen and scouts operated.

In all, there were 34 veterinary officers, 59 veterinary assistants and 300 stockmen.

Supporting facilities in disease diagnosis and vaccine production were established. These included disease research and diagnostic laboratories in Juba and Wau, and a veterinary assistants' school at Malakal. The modern laboratories were built, equipped and managed through international aid as part of the rehabilitation of the south after the end of the first civil war.

All three facilities — the two laboratories and the school — are non-functional now.

Disease has always been a major limiting factor in southern Sudan's livestock production system. Disease control measures, even during the peace period, were inadequate and underdeveloped. Examining the two major cattle diseases helps to emphasise the gravity of the disease factor ...

Rinderpest is endemic in southern Sudan, especially in the flood plains. Outbreaks were reported along the Sudan-Ethiopian border with a large one occurring among Dinka and Nuer cattle in 1980, with a daily crude mortality rate of 1%.

Reliable information was unavailable then, and still is. Diagnosis was generally tentatively arrived at, rather than by laboratory means. A survey in 1982 in Bahr el Ghazal region established that 77.6% of animals sampled demonstrated antibodies against rinderpest. Vaccination campaigns had been undertaken from 1975 – 1979, but had only mustered an annual 15% coverage. The high immunity levels discovered in the survey were therefore partly attributed to vaccination — it was not possible in the field to identify which animals had been vaccinated — although it was agreed that most of the antibodies found were due to natural infection.

The second major cattle disease is chronic bovine pleuropneumonia (CBPP). This is an endemic disease with many outbreaks in the past, although acute cases were rare. In the same 1982 survey in Bahr el Ghazal, 17.2% of examined cattle were found positive and estimates put the total infection rate at up to 40%.

Infected animals usually become carriers and are a potential source of widespread and fatal epidemics. This is so because in adverse conditions of stress like starvation, long trekking and resultant exhaustion, the cattle relapse and become active CBPP carriers.

The present civil strife therefore provides a ripe set of conditions for major epidemics of CBPP to flare up.

Throughout this same period of peace, staff development programmes were implemented by the government with international help, to alleviate the serious manpower shortage in improving the livestock sector and providing more protein for the Sudanese. These programmes were a success until the non-governmental organisations started pulling out of the south at the outset of the war. A trickle of people is now being trained abroad.

Livestock marketing was organised privately: the government only provided auction yards in the major towns, and poor slaughterhouse facilities. Cattle were trekked to consuming centres from producing areas over long distances ranging from 100 – 700 kilometres (60 – 440 miles).

Since 1983 ...

Because the war's major proponents were and are initially from the Nilotic, Dinka and Nuer, and later the Shilluk and other ethnic groups from southern Sudan, the main destructive consequences are being experienced in the flood plains — which are the major cattle-producing areas of the region.

Most veterinary facilities have come to a dead stop. One can say that only limited livestock services are operative in the major southern towns of Juba, Wau, Malakal, and other district headquarters which have not fallen into the hands of the SPLA.

Within these areas or centres, the cattle population is negligible compared with the overall stock population. In and around Juba, for example, there are an estimated 50,000 to 60,000 head of cattle which enjoy relative health care. The Terekeka district, with an estimated cattle population of about 500,000, has some community-based animal health services. About 320,000 head of cattle have been vaccinated against rinderpest/CBPP — that is, no more than about 4% of the total cattle population in the south.

Average prices for cattle, sheep and goats have gone up eight times or more since 1983/84 in Juba town. At the time of writing in mid-1988, a 250 kilogram (550 lbs) steer costs about £S1,200 (US$300) compared with £S150 (US$37.50) in 1982/83. Fewer cattle are presented at the Juba auction yard, making meat more expensive for town dwellers in Equatoria.

The table shows average cattle sales and their prices for 1982/83 and 1987/88.

AVERAGE CATTLE SALES (Nos) AND THEIR AVERAGE PRICES FOR 1982/83 – 1987/88.

Type of animal	Average monthly sales		Average prices per head	
	1982/83	1987/88	1982/83	1987/88
Bulls	540	549	£S150.00	£S1,200.00
Steer	644	–	£S150.00	–
Cows	31,943	463	£S190.00	–
Heifer	28,346	–	£S250.00	–

Sources: Project Development Unit and Juba Area Council.

The figures for cows are higher because most of the cows auctioned went to the slaughterhouse rather than for breeding. In most instances, the ages of cows sold ranged between 10 and 15 years.

In spite of attempts to learn about the other regions — Bahr el Ghazal and Upper Nile — valid data has been hard to come by. It is anybody's guess as to what is happening to the cattle in most of the production areas.

The war has taken its toll of buildings, vehicles, equipment and personnel. Only Equatoria region, which as it happens has the most livestock personnel, still retains staff. Elsewhere, staff have split between the regional government, the SPLA/SPLM, and Khartoum.

The war has also had a grave effect on the use of vaccines. Since 1983, for example, 514,600 doses of rinderpest vaccines have been hoarded because they could not be used. Some of these were earmarked for Bahr el Ghazal and Upper Nile: they could not be

Thor Ullerø/Norwegian Church Aid

Digging a shallow well for cattle.

transported to their destinations because of security limitations. At the same time, the quantity of CBPP vaccine received was inadequate and therefore very little was done in the way of vaccination: 32,000 doses were received and 15,000 doses used.

From 1982/83 to 1987/88, a total of 591,000 millilitres of antibiotics were received — enough to treat only 7,880 head of cattle.

The few cars for staff are either more than 10 years old and in poor condition, or are usually unusable because of shortages of fuel and spare parts.

Before war broke out again in 1983, two livestock improvement projects had been established with international aid and stocked with imported cattle with the aim of introducing into the local herds — the zebu breed — a hybrid gene for increased production in milk and meat. The farms were also to serve as models for improved management practices.

One of the farms, at Juba Bilinyang, still functions, but with difficulty. Most of the 25 or so of those who acquired imported breeds or their crosses have lost them due to insecurity (they were taken by the SPLA), the East Coast Fever epidemic of 1986 and lack of drugs.

The second project, at Marial Bai, Wau, prided itself by 1983 on having more than 600 exotic dairy cattle and over 1,000 zebu cattle. Nothing exists now. The animals were either distributed to senior government officials and perished, or fell prey to the SPLA.

Disturbed cycle

The war has greatly disturbed the traditional cycle of animal husbandry, and has led to abnormal stock movements: pastoralists are forced to take their cattle to areas unsuitable for livestock. This involves trekking long distances. Stock are exposed to starvation, thirst and general stress.

The pastoralists, who over time immemorial developed strong attitudes towards herd management, do not have enough time and peace to give needed care to their stock.

The negative effect of the war on the growth rate of stock is difficult to assess. It is, of course, quite apparent that sales have dwindled since the war started because production areas are cut off from major consuming centres. On the other hand, losses due to diseases must have increased because of a complete lack of veterinary services, vaccines and drugs in the rural areas. Other losses include cattle indiscriminately eaten by rebel forces, or lost to the government army and militias. An unknown number must also been eaten by the owners to avert starvation.

Most pastoralists' families have broken down. Husbands, wives and even children have been separated, some forever. Young men who normally look after cattle have either joined the SPLA (at will or force of circumstances) or fled to safety zones in the north.

Those who have gone to urban centres have adapted to town life — thus losing their traditional skills. Tribal marriages have become difficult to perform due to dislocation of people and lack of stock — which is the only traditionally accepted dowry payment. Young women have been introduced into town life and circumstances there have forced them into prostitution and other frowned-on activities.

In peaceful times, pastoralists traded some of their stock to purchase basic necessities like salt, onions, cooking oil and essential drugs for their cattle. Most dramatically, in the 11 years of peace, the pastoralists who previously walked naked in the rural areas were transformed and adorned themselves in colourful clothing. Cattle provided the cash for this great change.

The war has reversed all these achievements. We learn of a pastoralist rural population which is deprived of food and goes unclothed. It is a population which, in the absence of modern drugs, cannot treat their revered cattle but must watch them die in agony.

The security implications of the war for pastoralists are profound, particularly because most of the people are armed. Armed tribal groups have looted, raided and killed their neighbours, in incidents involving Dinka versus Mundari, Dinka versus Nuer, Bagara Arabs versus Dinka, Toposa versus Buya and Latuko. Most disturbingly, the Toposa in the Sudan have rustled cattle from the Turkana of Kenya. This last episode, which occurred in 1988, caused a diplomatic row between Kenya and Sudan.

For a long time we are going to see intersectional, intertribal and interstate mini-warfare involving disputes over grazing land, cattle rustling and vendetta missions.

The Mundari experience

One of the most affected districts in Equatoria region, and one for which there is some information, is Terekeka. About 80 miles north of Juba, it has an estimated 80,000 people and 500,000 head of livestock.

The economy of the Mundari, the tribe which inhabits the district, is based on sedentary cultivation in scattered homesteads with a transhumant livestock system.

Between December 1984 and April 1985, the Mundari were attacked by the SPLA forces, mainly because of their neutrality and non-involvement in the war and because they were an obstacle to the onward advance of the rebels towards Juba, the capital of Equatoria.

Poorly defended, their villages were burnt, cattle and granaries were looted, and innocent people killed.

The Mundari were forced out of their homesteads and moved to the south and south-west into rangeland normally unsuited for livestock. Removal saved some of the cattle but important crop-producing areas were lost.

Some stability returned to the district after government army action and defence preparation by the Mundari.

But loss of crops and producing areas resulted in widespread famine. The natives were forced to sell some of their livestock for food at giveaway prices.

In order to save the valuable stock from being sold for food, and help reallocate the stock within the district, the British non-governmental organisation, Oxfam, started a restocking programme using food exchanged for animals. The exchanged animals were given to people who had lost all their stock to the rebels and government reprisals.

After about 30 families had been restocked, the programme was interrupted when the district was again invaded in June 1986.

The Mundari were forced to flee to Juba with their remaining cattle, totalling about 50,000, leaving behind their modest but important assets.

At the time of the influx into Juba, veterinary services were minimal and a lot of the Mundari cattle died from an unidentified disease. A mass vaccination with haemorrhagic septicaemia and blackquarter vaccine was started, but failed to control it. Massive slaughtering was a common sight in Juba town, where carcasses were hawked around for sale — they were termed "postmortem meat".

Most of the cattle-owners affected say that this has been the worst disease epidemic in their lifetime.

Some individuals lost as many as 30% of their stock; about 15% of the Mundari lost all their livestock through the disease combined with other adverse factors.

The disease, which has no known traditional name and remedy, is now being referred to as "Juba disease". All known traditional medicines were tried without success.

In December 1986, the disease was confirmed as East Coast Fever. Oxfam responded by providing the drug needed for the disease. At the time of writing in July 1988, 1,400 head of cattle have been successfully treated against the disease with less than 1% mortality.

Wendy Wallace

The people who lost most or all of their animals have been forced into different levels of destitution. This has seriously affected the nutritional status of children. About 17,000 Mundari were forced into camps, and others into doing odd jobs to generate income to meet their basic daily needs.

The damage done

The war has taken its toll and continues to do so; until when, only the warring parties can determine. It is too much and too early to ask anyone to assess and quantify the damage done until now and to come up with a comprehensive picture of the war's effects on future negative development of pastoralism in the southern Sudan.

Suffice to say that the damage already done is very profound and tragic.

Accurate information is unavailable. We have just managed, with limited figures, to patch up a short story to present to the world. Others who live until the end of the war might be lucky and succeed, although with difficulty, in presenting a more justifiable and scientific version of this tragedy.

There will be a lot to do, and much money to spend, in order to rehabilitate the pastoral industry at the end of the war.

But for the present, our attention should be directed, wherever conditions permit, to the plight of the innocent people and those who have been caught in a war they cannot fully comprehend.

Efforts should be made to provide drugs and vaccines to inaccessible areas. But who among the warring parties can appreciate this?

This is not the normal summary that follows a well-conceived and researched paper.

We hope you will bear with us.

It is late-afternoon at the Akori cattle camp, about 15 kilometres (10 miles) out of Juba, and the cattle are coming in from grazing. There are 300 to 400 people in the camp.
The man we talk to is 40 to 50 years old; he is the head of the cattle camp. Most of the elders gather round to listen.

"My name is Idja Anok," he says, "but I have another name of warriorship, the name of somebody who has killed a cow that is spotted like a leopard.

How long have you been in this camp?
I have lived here two years now, because of the insecurity at home, in Paguere, home of Chief Mayom. It is four years since I left Paguere.

We were attacked: my cattle were taken and I was caught. I was tied from a tree to hang. When friends released me later, I looked for the remainder of my cattle and ran away. Since that time I have been wandering around for four years, but just two years here around Juba district.

Who attacked you?
It is Garang's people who are chasing us. They came and told us that our ancestors had no cattle. 'We are taking all these cattle back this year', they said. 'You go back to agriculture — dig with the hoe, make granaries. If you don't do that, you will die', they said. 'We are not leaving you any cattle.'

So did you lose all your cattle?
Fifty cattle were taken. I managed to come here with two, but fifty cattle were forced out of me at Paguere.

How many other people moved with you?
All these people you see here were with me originally at Paguere and we moved together. All of them were running from the same troubles. In our wanderings all of us were together, but many others were killed, as we went round looking for safety.

Have you been back to the area where you came from?
I have never gone back. If you are hanged in a tree do you really think of going back? I just want to stay around here with my few cattle so that they can multiply in peace, far away from trouble.

But it seems that some people have stayed there ...
Those people are staying there with a lot of sacrifice. When the time comes for milking, the enemies will come around to tax them. They must fill a jerkin, like this one, full of milk which the SPLA take, plus a gourd like this one here, full of milk also. The whole cattle camp might raise 10 jerkins in just one evening, while their children are dying. There is a lot of death because of this SPLA tax. Every day, if it is not milk during daytime, the enemy come and bleed the fat cattle; many cattle now have swollen necks, because of the blood being drained from them. Sometimes, because they have finished all the big bulls, they kill very tiny bulls who might not have stopped suckling their mothers.

If you try to go away and you are found, you will be pushed back and many, many of your cattle will be taken as a fine.

But I have been suffering around here, too. I am chased by my hosts: 'Go out of here'. I move on again and people tell me: 'Go away from here, we don't like you with your cattle'.

So I have been moving round, round, round — but I don't think it will be safe for me to go back to Paguere.

What do you think the problem is with the local people here?
I think it is likely that the cattle are the source of the hatred of local people against us. We are people who ran away from danger: we wouldn't think any honest people here would just hit us — we are looking for safety. So it is likely that the cattle are the source of the jealousy.

When we take our cattle for grazing, the cattle will sometimes trespass over crop fields. Once this is done, even if the place is so small, the owners will call for the army; the army will command us to pay fines which go as high as £S1,000 (US$250). Sometimes crops may not even be there, but if the place is a bit dark and the cattle pass over, then we are accused of grazing our cattle on crops. We often have to sell cattle to meet these fines.

The other thing is that the local people tell us that we are pulling the enemy towards them. The SPLA are looking for our cattle to eat; if we are sighted with our cattle, they will definitely follow us. It means we will have brought trouble to the local people.

They are not happy with this — that is why they say, 'You must go away from here, we don't like you to be near us here', and they cause every kind of excuse so as to get us in trouble with the army and the police, so that we are moved away from them.

This year the rains seem to be good. Does that mean that you will be able to graze around this area for quite a long time without any problem?
It is very difficult. How would we manage to cultivate when we stay in a place for five days until the problems become too many and we have to move to another place? We go six miles or so and again the people of that area will cause us so many

fines, so many troubles daily. We are all kept moving. And, anyway, if we were to plant crops, it might even increase the problems we meet from the local people.

Is there any form of taxation that the government is able to get from you here, now that you are near the town?
We don't pay any. If the government did ask for something, we would not be able to pay. How would we manage to meet demands for taxes at the moment when people are suffering, people are dying, people are being chased from place to place? In the past, we could cultivate at home, we could raise some money from our cattle and we were able to pay. But now, we couldn't meet any demands for paying taxes.

Most of the young men and the boys are here now, but we don't see many women. Are they here?
Many of them are around. During daytime, some of them go to the nearby markets to see if they can get anything to bring here. Some of them go to look for a type of greens in the forest. They also prick the healthy cattle in the neck to get the blood, and then they cook it together with the greens from the forest, and we eat this with the milk.

But this is unusual to have women with you at the cattle camp......
In the past, yes. We the elders and our women would stay at home to dig and cultivate in the village. But in this present insecure time, no-one would be able to stay in peace at home. Here now, you will find the girl, the woman, as well as the man.

If we are able to find a way of bringing everyone from the village, they must all be here, so that we are safe. We must keep seeds for the future. We can't leave anybody around to be killed.

We are getting trouble with our cattle here, but we have no choice. We will have to stay here. We are not going back there, as long as the situation continues to be unsafe for us."

Jon Bennett and Joseph Abuk

Robert Lubajo works with the Regional Directorate of Forestry in Equatoria region.

"Remember in 1986 when the Mundari tribesmen were chased away from Terekeka and had to flee for their lives? They were settled here, at the foot of this hill. But within a very short time, they carried out a massive destruction of the forest cover here.

In the last three years, a lot has happened to the forest in and around Juba. Before 1983, the area about five kilometres (three miles) from here used to be covered with a thick forest of acacias and other species. But now you cannot find any appreciable forest cover before Luri River, on the western side of Luri hill.

This means that, in just three years, the forest has moved a distance of six kilometres (4 miles). This is a very great reduction in the forest cover.

Before 1983, that is, before the war in the south, the area beside the road here was settled by people who came seasonally from Juba town to cultivate. Beyond that, let's say three or four kilometres (about two miles) away, it was just a jungle with occasional cattle-grazers coming in the wet season to graze their animals; in the dry season, they would move towards the river at night. There was a lot of tree cover, a lot of forest.

But now the forest has disappeared. It goes without saying that this problem has been mainly caused by the increased number of displaced persons who have cut the trees, mostly for firewood and building materials.

Very often we apprehend people. We try to arrest them but, when we interview them, we find out that they are people who are helpless, they have nothing, they have no source of income, they have nowhere to sleep except the displaced camps.

The trouble is that there are many categories of displaced persons. We have able-bodied people who cut trees to make charcoal and also to extract poles for sale in Juba market, so that they can buy the necessities of life.

Then we have the able-bodied women who tend to cut those trees that are trying to regenerate, the saplings. And then there are the small girls and the old ladies who will come and even remove the twigs and sometimes even the stumps of the trees that are left in the ground; they dig them up because they do not have the strength to walk long distances.

And the problem is mounting daily. Because of the insecurity, it is not safe to go more than a few kilometres away from Juba. That's one thing. And the second thing is that old people and the young cannot travel long distances — many of them are hungry. They can't really go into the bush where they might find wood that can be cut, even if they were adventurous enough to do that.

But there are other strong people who are braver and they sometimes venture into the bush areas where they are likely to meet the rebels.

There used to be three categories of law enforcement officers. One was the village chief, who could arrest and levy fines on anyone destroying trees. The second was the wildlife officer, but they were restricted to areas that had wildlife reserves and forest reserves. The third one was the forest department, both the regional forest department and the district forest office; these had the power to arrest and to correct people.

But now all of these law enforcement officers have more or less ceased to function. Most of them cannot move far from town, because of the insecurity. Many of the wildlife posts that were outside Juba have been closed down because of insecurity and their forces have been co-opted into the army. I am right now trying to carry out a rehabilitation project here. We are reforesting the area. Where the trees are not regenerating, we plant more. Where they are regenerating, we try to protect them. We try to plant species that are not palatable to animals — like the neem, which is a bitter species and goats don't like it. For those species which are very palatable to animals, we plant a few at a time and we try to erect protective thorny structures around them.

But we are not planting everywhere. We have just planted five hectares — we do not have enough seedlings."

REFUGEES: AN ASSET NOT A BURDEN

PETER VAN KRIEKEN

Dr Peter van Krieken holds a PhD in international law. He joined UNHCR in 1975 and served in Beirut, Sana'a, Addis Ababa and Zirndorf, West Germany. From 1983-87, he was director of the Netherlands Refugee Foundation, SV999. Since 1987, Dr van Krieken has served as head of the UNHCR southern Sudan programme, based in Juba. He writes here in a personal capacity.

For most of them, this is their second war. Their first war, in the form of civil strife, forced them to leave Uganda and to settle in south Sudan.

Yet the turmoil of Sudan's current civil war might uproot them all once again. And if this happens, it would have almost unique consequences. For these refugees from Uganda have not been a burden to the country of asylum, Sudan, but an asset; their departure would add to the economic collapse of the Equatoria province.

A refugee is someone who has crossed an international border. Originally, refugees were defined as people who had left their country with a "well-founded fear of being persecuted". That is how the 1951 Refugee Convention describes it. The persecution has to be linked to political opinion, religion, race, social group or nationality.

It is indeed a beautiful definition. But is it able to cope with reality on the African continent? Hardly — and it was in this light a wise move that the Organisation of African Unity insisted in 1969 on its own Refugee Convention in which due attention is paid to victims of aggression, civil war and other man-made disasters.

It goes without saying that, in the case of the Ugandans, their fleeing from the Amin, Obote and Okello regimes means that we deal with clearcut refugees.

By limiting ourselves to Ugandan refugees, we shall *not* focus on: internally displaced southerners (now in the towns of Juba and Yei); southerners who moved to the north, to the capital of Khartoum; southerners who have taken refuge in Ethiopia — some 300,000 people; Equatorians seeking refuge in northern Uganda — by early 1988, about 10,000 had already gone there.

Most of the Ugandans started coming to south Sudan after 1979. In 1984/1985 their numbers had risen to 250,000. Many lived in so-called self-settled areas. Some — 150,000 of them — lived in 20 settlements on the East Bank (north of Nimule) and 30 on the West Bank (Yei River district in Maridi area).

About 50,000 left as a result of the April/May 1986 events when groups of armed men attacked people in East Bank settlements. This coincided with the coming to power in Uganda of President Museveni.

The repatriation process continued gradually. By April 1988 some 85,000 Ugandans were still in south Sudan (in Juba, Yei and Maridi), but many of them were still planning to return home. Some others — members of the Acholi tribe — will probably continue to remain in south Sudan until the situation in their area of origin has been normalised.

Painting a triptych

One can describe the Ugandan/south Sudan ordeal as a triptych — a painting with three panels — representing, from left to right, yesterday, today, tomorrow.

YESTERDAY: the south Sudanese who themselves fled as refugees to Uganda during the 1955 – 72 civil war. They were educated and trained in Uganda, and came home with, for example, a new set of agricultural techniques.

TODAY: the main panel reflects the impact of the presence of the Ugandans, with their excellent educational, agricultural and marketing skills they have boosted the areas where they settled.

Wendy Wallace

Ugandan refugee settlement in Equatoria, 1982.

TOMORROW: The third panel shows a devastated area, demolished by turmoil and strife and deprived of the asset the refugees had proved to be. Moreover, people from the Sudan region of Equatoria are now bound to leave in great numbers for Uganda. It can be emphasised that this "mutual exchange" of refugees between Sudan and Uganda has contributed greatly to regional integration and mutual appreciation, a point often overlooked in debates on relations between the countries concerned.

What turned the southern Sudan refugee exercise into a success story? These factors have played a major role:

— availability of land;
— a good, fertile climate;
— the hospitable attitude of the local population ("we know what it is to be a refugee; we were refugees ourselves");
— the co-operation of the local authorities;
— a well-devised plan of action carried out;
— excellent implementing agencies.

The refugees came in gradually, not in one sudden move. This gave refugee organisations time to do a decent job, and to learn from experience. The first settlement came into being in 1979, the most recent one in 1984.

It is worth noting that a polemic developed in the world of refugee workers, as some considered the settlement structure too authoritarian. One phrase used to describe this was "imposing aid". A more libertarian approach would have yielded better results, they claimed.

Others doubt it, and feel supported by observations made during the 1987-88 repatriation effort: people from the settlements appear to be better off generally, as with their harvest, education, health and personal belongings, than if they had not been in settlements.

However, it should be stressed that a refugee-assistance programme is different from a normal development programme in outlook, pace, goals and methodology.

Refugee successes

The refugees have achieved some notable successes ...

These days, in 1988, every convoy arriving in Juba is greeted with great enthusiasm and great relief. It brings cement, diesel, lubricants, beer — and above all, badly needed food. The food, from East Africa, is invariably for the relief programmes.

The limited supply of food pushes prices up to prohibitive levels. Thus supplies of "commercial food" are of the utmost importance. There is no exaggeration in stating that up to two thirds of the "commercial food" has been produced by the refugees: recipients have turned into producers; former receivers of relief food have turned their plots of lands into the main grain-basket of Equatoria.

A second success relates to education. All the settlements had schools and a great percentage of the school-aged children indeed attended school. Almost a quarter of the pupils were Sudanese from neighbouring villages and 90% of the teachers were Ugandans. This means that the local population had a net benefit from the presence of refugees in their area. A similar story could be told about dispensaries, clinics, and marketing.

Attending school is not automatic. I met Tiko Betty Ajonye in one of the settlements in June 1986; she was 12 at the time. Her father, formerly a post office clerk in Arua, northern Uganda, was away during the week undergoing a teacher training course. The whereabouts of her mother (if she was still alive) were unknown.

Betty attended Intermediate 2. She was very bright. But who looked after Florence, Joyce, Grace and Charles, her younger brother and sisters? Who took them to primary school, who prepared their breakfast, their evening meal? Who fetched the water, worked the land, did the laundry? Indeed, it was 12-year-old Betty who, apart from being a schoolgirl, ran a whole household.

Success doesn't come easily: it is to do with tears, sweat, discipline and courage. But in 1988, Betty successfully sat for her Intermediate final examination.

At a third level of success, many of the refugees have contributed to the general economic effort of Equatoria. Most of them have done so as farmers, but in fact you can see Ugandans everywhere: as teacher at Yei Day, as accountant, as secretary, as lecturer at Juba University, as liaison officer, etc. Indeed, a certain jealousy developed in the area towards the refugees, over jobs.

Wendy Wallace

Ugandan refugee building his home in Equatoria in 1983.

Refugees are widely considered as a problem in themselves. That is a wrong attitude. More often than not refugees bring skills with them, and areas of asylum enjoy their added value. This is certainly the case with Ugandan refugees in southern Sudan. They came from a country which, for example, had many more years of experience in regard to education and the economy. This extra experience also accounted for the easy integration and/or settlement of many urban Ugandan refugees in towns like Kajo Kaji, Yei and Juba.

The most important feature of the successful settlement/integration (UNCHR generally talks about "local integration": the less pretentious term "local settlement" may be more apt), is the almost complete absence of resettlement efforts — that is, settlement in a third country.

The international community, or at least the potential immigration countries like the United States, Canada or Australia, neither perceived nor conceived of the Ugandan refugees as potential immigrants. Moreover, neither the Ugandans — nor the NGOs, for that matter — were pushing for resettlement. This meant that a more or less normal community structure remained intact, enabling the community to become self-sufficient quite quickly.

It should be stressed that resettlement yields many negative vibes: the settlement becomes a long-term clearing house, the commitment to the immediate future is far from 100%, and moreover the natural leaders are often the first to be accepted for resettlement.

Returning home is best

The week preceding Easter 1988 was eventful. The Juba-Nile-Bridge, the vital link between the East and West Banks, was nearly blown up. A convoy arrived in Juba with 250 local trucks carrying food from the refugee-populated areas near Maridi; also, a UNHCR truck limped in: four bullet-holes were witness to the ambush which the convoys had to go through. A Ugandan delegation visited Yei and Juba, urging the refugees to walk home, rather than passively waiting for transport possibilities.

The most striking event of that very week was the arrival of the

Torit convoy, which had taken 10 days to cover the 80 miles from Torit to Juba. The passengers — 80 trucks and 3,000-4,000 people walking — had to go through a great ordeal: lack of water, plus bullets and landmines which had taken the lives of more than 70 people. Moreover, those cruel anti-personnel mines had blown off the legs of many an innocent traveller.

These events had an impact on the decisionmaking process of those who were in charge of the repatriation programme, and of those who were considering repatriation.

In refugee literature three forms of durable solutions appear to feature: local settlement, resettlement and repatriation.

In the case of Ugandans in southern Sudan, resettlement was not at stake; local settlement was successful; yet repatriation is always considered the most ideal durable solution.

Civil strife or not, successful local settlement or not, if repatriation is a viable alternative, it is worth pursuing: returning home is the ultimate goal in a refugee's life.

It should be emphasised that the civil strife in the Sudan was just one of the factors forcing or enabling the refugees to go home. It may be recalled that when Uganda's NRM-government came into power early in 1986, Museveni managed to introduce a new spirit into his country, combined with discipline, new initiatives and a positive outlook. It was understandable that many refugees decided to go home.

The southern Sudan civil strife, I submit, upset the repatriation programme, speeding up the return of some and delaying it for others; but it can in no way be considered the decisive element in the process of refugees making up their minds.

The armed 'visits'

In April and May 1986, some settlements on the East Bank were "visited" — forced entry by armed men, sometimes just a couple, sometimes as many as 50, normally in some kind of uniform.

Those spring visits were shocking to many. Irrespective of what really happened — some beating, robbing, looting, with a total of two or three refugees killed — the whole of the East Bank became upset and a massive exodus resulted. Was it repression, the assault

Wendy Wallace

in itself, or rather fear because of stories which grew out of proportion?

The actual momentum of the exodus does not need to be denied. A question mark remains concerning the reasons for their decision. In this respect it is worth noting that research is still going on as to the reasons why Palestinians left their villages in 1948.

The flow of repatriation was also affected by bureaucracy and related (political?) decisions. At one point during the southern Sudan repatriation programme, a government decision was taken, ordering that the names of all those being repatriated had to be submitted to the Ugandan authorities in Kampala. Only upon the latter's formal acknowledgement could repatriation proceed.

In an area where convoys between the main towns, Juba and Yei, take place once a month and where computers and word processors have not yet entered the scene, these kinds of requirements result in an effective standstill of the operations.

On other occasions (fatal) events in northern Uganda forced UNHCR Uganda to suspend the programme. Moreover, the Yei-Kaya road, the only remaining link between Sudan and Uganda, was often mined and/or ambushed. Convoys could not be frequently organised, as escorts were not always available.

A highlight was undoubtedly President Museveni's letter to the refugees. He, in fact, was of the opinion that a walk back to Uganda could and should be organised. In normal times such a walk is quite feasible and even has symbolic value.

In times of war all unnecessary risks should be avoided. The organisation of such a walk was considered by many a nightmare, both logistically and in regard to security.

Events sometimes overtake ideas, plans, preparations. At the time the trucks started rolling massively — on Easter Sunday 1988, a convoy with more than 7,500 refugees on 90 trucks left Yei for Uganda — the refugee area was struck by a measles epidemic.

Many of the refugee areas had become inaccessible, due to the war. Even medical teams had been unable to visit the areas concerned. This resulted in a considerable delay in the immunisation programme. Moreover, (an accident never comes alone) at a time when many refugees were forced (by the many, often atrocious assaults on their settlements) to move to Yei town, that very town happened to have run out of measles vaccine. The results were destructive: at least 40 deaths.

The civil war in southern Sudan has had a tremendous, often traumatic, impact on the refugees who found refuge there. The settlements were visited. People were robbed, looted, beaten, raped or killed. Some were beheaded or hanged from trees. Fear prevailed. Refugees became uprooted once again.

It takes a year to rebuild what one month of fighting destroys. It often takes a lifetime to recover from traumatic experiences.

The story of Alice: Probably the best way to describe the situation in southern Sudan, in early 1988, is by introducing Alice.

Alice was a Ugandan refugee, an 18-year-old secondary school pupil. She attended school in Juba. The rest of her family was in Pajok, some 120 miles from Juba on the East Bank.

I met Alice when she was a patient in the Juba Teaching Hospital. Her medical evacuation was recommended. But before sending her to Khartoum or Nairobi, we decided to send a blood sample to Nairobi for testing.

A radio message arrived shortly afterwards, confirming our fears: Alice was terminally ill. Her father didn't give up. He asked me to send a message to Pajok. He was convinced that Alice's illness was linked to a mistake made during the arrangements for her wedding. The dowry was not enough. The father wanted his family to slaughter two cows, to make up for the mistake.

What could I do but convey the message: one should never deprive someone else of the idea that he has done everything to save his daughter's life.

Upon transmitting the message, Pajok station was a couple of days off the air. A defective radio, a flat battery?

Reality was different. Pajok had been attacked by the SPLA. The radio man, Robert, had escaped into the bush — and had taken the radio with him to keep it safe. After he returned, he reported Pajok was in serious trouble: cattle had been seized, huts and granaries put on fire.

Alice's family was just one of the many families who suffered in the attack. On top of that, one of her brothers was killed. No cattle were left for any reconciliatory slaughter.

Alice passed away shortly afterwards.

WOMEN — NOW THE SOLE BREADWINNERS

MARY WANI

Mary Hillary Wani joined the Ministry of Finance and Economic Affairs in Juba as a bookkeeper in 1976. Two years later, she won a scholarship to the University of Juba and graduated in 1982 with a BSc in accounting. She then returned to the ministry as an Inspector of accounts. From 1983– 85, she worked as an accountant with the West German relief agency GTZ. In 1986, she enrolled at Khartoum University where she obtained a diploma in development planning. She is currently studying for her MA in development planning.

The instability in the south has had many undesirable effects for the whole southern community; but women are the worst-hit because of their special role in feeding rural households.

As in most parts of Africa, women in southern Sudan do more than 80% of the farm work. Within households there is a clearcut division of labour: the men are primarily responsible for clearing and land preparation, whereas planting is carried out by all members of the family, including women. Weeding is done exclusively by women. Harvesting is also the concern of women. Crop processing, too, is done mainly by women: grain, vegetables and pulses are dried and winnowed ready for storage in granaries.

In the pastoral areas, the basis of subsistence is milk derived from herds, but many people also carry out sporadic cultivation to supplement their food. Women particularly are fulltime cultivators whereas most men manage the group's livestock in the traditional manner. Processing milk products such as yoghurt and fat is done mainly by women.

In addition to farm work, southern women are the fuel-gatherers and water-fetchers. Along river banks and around towns, women are engaged in vegetable growing, which is an important economic activity. The production, marketing and management of the earnings are entirely women's tasks and under their control. This is also the case for small-scale poultry keeping.

But due to the insecurity and widespread hunger, the population of the south has become mobile. In the remote rural areas, entire villages have gone into hiding, scattered in small households deep in the bush. As a result of this migration to new areas, land clearance and preparation consume much of the time — and always with the danger that the new land may not be fertile enough for agriculture and the yields may be low.

Collecting firewood and fetching water, traditionally simple tasks as children can assist their elders, also pose a problem now. For those women who remain in the rural areas, moving around in the bush collecting firewood or fetching water from the river is very risky as they might run into the SPLA or the national army forces. The encounter can be disastrous.

Missionary education

Formal education was introduced to the south by missionaries during Anglo-Egyptian rule. There was no clear educational policy, and the various missions worked on their own without government control or supervision. The social and cultural attitudes of the time did not favour the education of children, let alone that of girls. The attitudes kept many girls out of school. Right up to today, women in the south are in most cases the last to be sent to school and the first to be taken out.

Before the current war, the government established many schools in the south's rural areas and towns. Others were set up on a self-help basis. But there were never enough schools: progress was hampered by lack of trained manpower, shortage of materials and insufficient finance to meet the running costs.

The results are seen in Sudan's low literacy rates: about 80% of

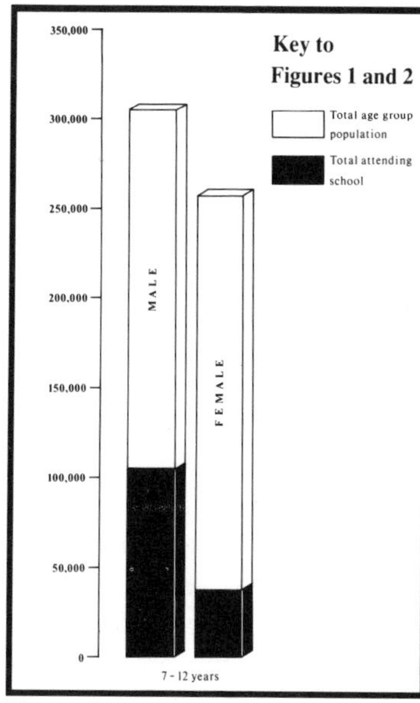

Figure 1.

people are illiterate, and this rises to 90% among women.

Figures 1 and 2 show the educational statistics for the southern region in the academic year 1980/81 — the most recent breakdown this writer could find.

It is apparent from the figures that the greater part of the populace is not attending school. But it can also be seen that female students are represented by a far lower percentage compared with male students. On average they are only a quarter of the total number of students in all the levels.

At present, the majority of schools in the south are non-operative as a result of the state of insecurity. The majority of children, in both rural areas and towns, are not at school. Only a small number of schools are open, in the major towns.

This state of affairs will in the long run lead to a decrease in the literacy rates achieved. Even those southerners who have migrated to the northern part of the country are no better off. They are economically disadvantaged and their children have no access to education. With the war persisting these children will be growing up without any basic education and without

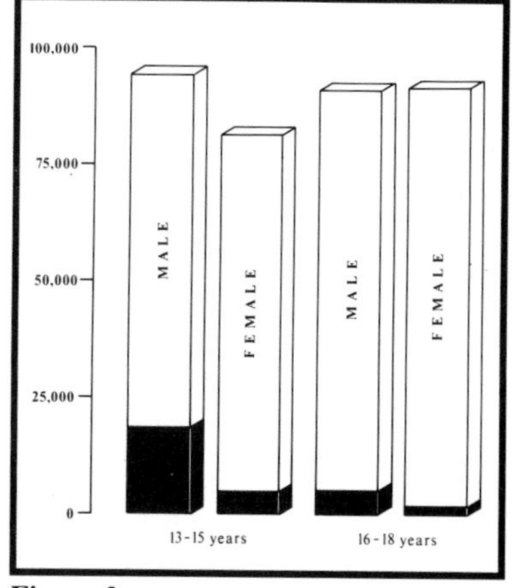

Figure 2.

any future prospects. For women, the literacy rates are likely to decrease drastically, and more and more women will be illiterate.

Women's organisations collapse

Women were first organised in the south under the Sudan Women Union. Each locality had its own group. The women were engaged in many activities such as nurseries, training in handicraft, needlework and sewing. Centres were established in the towns to cater for these activities; the rural areas were not involved. The membership was not wide, and the majority of the women who participated were politically motivated.

Currently, activities in the centres have come to a standstill because of the fighting.

Another women's organisation, called Women Self-Help Development Committee, assisted in the financing and training of self-help groups engaged in income-generating activities such as handicrafts and vegetable gardens. This was intended to supplement family income, thus contributing to economic development and the general welfare of the community. With its head office in Yei, western Equatoria, it supervised and assisted many women's groups all over Equatoria province.

At present, however, this organisation is handicapped by the lack of transport and communication caused by the war. Co-ordination and supervision of the groups is rendered impossible. Another obstacle is the lack of materials required for the various activities.

In 1977 the Regional Ministry of Co-operatives and Rural Development in 1977 set up an Institute for Integrated Rural Development in Amadi, in western Equatoria. The institute offered a nine-month training programme for community development officers, youth officers, agricultural extension workers and social workers. It also trained women and girls in a range of nutrition, childcare and agricultural activities.

The institute trained people from all over the south and, had all gone well, its results would have been felt by now and many women would have benefited from its services. Unfortunately, its activities were also terminated due to the state of insecurity in the area.

Many church women's groups have emerged, organised in

Jeremy Hartley/Oxfam

"Women: the core-builders of future generations."

societies or co-operatives. Women are engaged in a variety of income-generating activities including handicraft and needlework. Some groups have opened shops for selling their products. Previously groups co-operated with other local groups, exchanging experiences and ideas; products from rural areas were channelled for marketing in the towns. But co-ordination is currently not possible and each group is confined to its own locality.

Most of the functioning groups are located in the urban centres. In almost all rural areas, women are still engaged in handicraft work, making baskets, mats and pottery. But they are not organised in groups; they work individually and in most cases production is not for the market.

Increased responsibility

As commonly happens in war situations, many southern Sudan households have lost their adult male members — they are directly involved in the war. Many households are headed by women because the men either migrate elsewhere or are killed in the war.

Thus women assume responsibility for the whole household. They become the breadwinner as well as catering for the family's domestic needs. This new role is highly demanding, in terms both of time and capability.

It becomes more difficult under the prevailing conditions, where people are always on the run. People are prompted to move from place to place in search of food and security. Many have fallen victims of the SPLA or the national army or even the local militia. So to survive one has to avoid any encounter with them.

Although women are traditionally the major agricultural food producers, they have become less and less able to produce enough food for their families without the assistance of their male partners in such heavy work as land clearance. Most households, in both rural and urban areas, are faced with starvation. In fact, cases of death associated with starvation are not uncommon.

Most of the economic activities practised by women, such as vegetable production, handicraft and the like are also disrupted by the war. The marketing of these products is not possible since most areas are cut off with no means of transport. This has deprived women of their extra income.

Another activity which constitutes a significant source of income for women in the south is the brewing of the local beer. This is practised mainly in towns. At present this activity is crippled in the south because of the lack of its major raw material, grain. Those women who have migrated to the north still brew beer: but they are doing it at the risk of being flogged and jailed if discovered by the police.

In short, the raging war in the south has incapacitated women economically.

This situation is made worse by the lack of medical services. Even before the war, health facilities in the south were inadequate: they were provided in the main urban centres but in rural areas were only available where some organisations were operating. Now, as a result of the instability, even those rural areas where health care units were established are closed. Women are soley dependent on whatever traditional health measures they have learnt, such as the use of herbs or the services of a traditional doctor or midwife.

Another problem brought by the war is prostitution. In the south

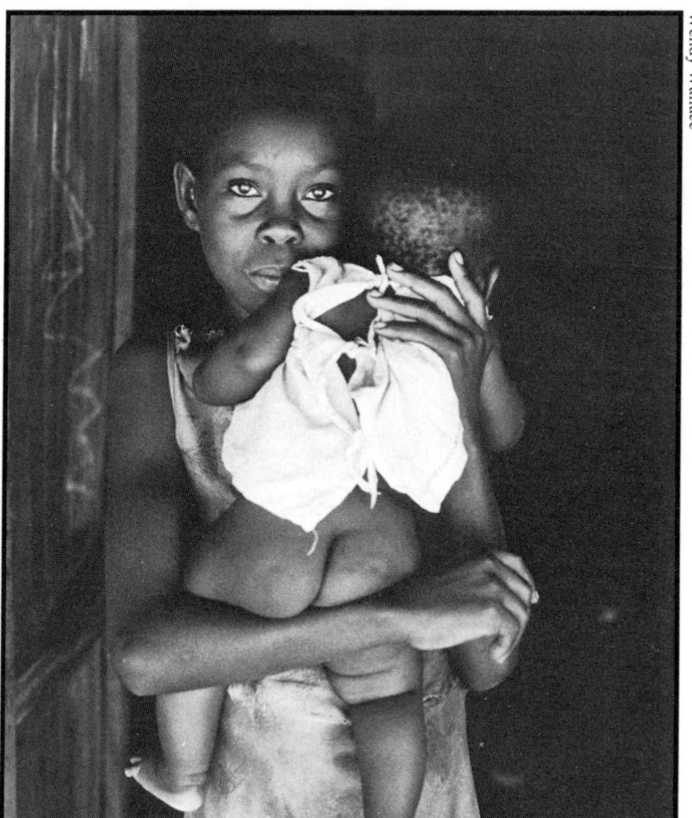

Wendy Wallace

The war increases women's responsibilities.

this practice is an urban phenomenon, unheard of in the rural communities.

Children leave families

The disintegration of families as a result of conditions created by the war has left on their own many young girls who would, under normal conditions, be under the care of older guardians. The maintenance of discipline in the house becomes difficult and many children break away from their families, especially when such basic needs as food are not provided. The mobility of women in search of food and security also subjects them to many hardships and as a result they become more vulnerable.

C Steele-Perkins/Magnum

The presence of the armed forces in the area contributes to the increase of such malpractices especially when it is soldiers who have access to food, as is the case in the south.

Many women have migrated from the rural areas to the major towns in the south. Others have migrated to the northern part of the country and the national capital in particular. Some have taken refuge in neighbouring countries.

However, the fate of these people is no better than that of those left behind in the south. They are residing in slums on the outskirts of towns. They have no reliable source of income but are dependent on whatever income they can get for their labour. Basic services such as water and health care are not available. The tasks of fetching water and collecting firewood have become more tedious and costly. Being in an urban centre and without any source of income, women are forced to walk long distances outside the town to collect firewood; some even resort to collecting small pieces of charcoal thrown away in garbage heaps. As for water, they have to buy it.

So to conclude, I would say that the state of instability in the south has inflicted very damaging effects on the whole southern community.

Both educational and health services are non-existent. Women are over-burdened by having to shoulder all the responsibility of their families in the absence of their male counterparts. All their economic activities are crippled. They are rendered incapable of producing food for their households.

The war has brought a host of social problems with which women have to cope. If the war continues, the south could lose much in terms of future human resources because women, who are the core-builders of future generations, are rendered helpless.

Nyamini is a camp for the Mundari pastoralist people displaced from Terekeka district. It is about 30 kilometres (20 miles) northwest of Juba.

"I am called Jakudu — I come from a place called Mayen. The SPLA have killed my husband. I have lost our properties, cattle and everything.

They killed him because they say that the Mundari are bad and because he was resisting over the cattle — he didn't want

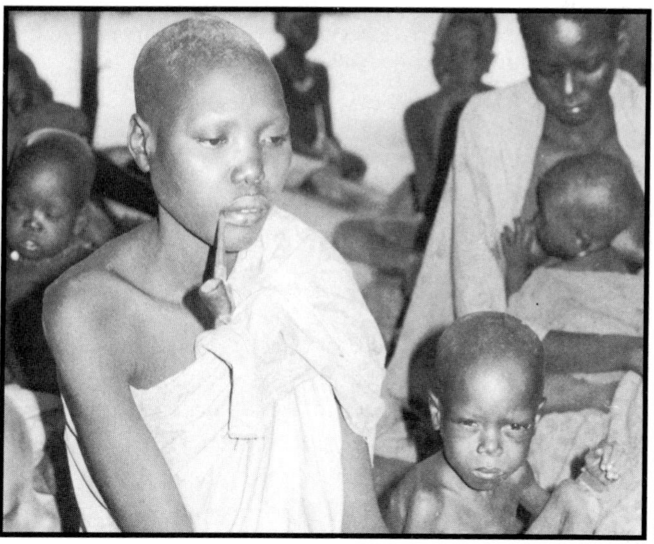

J. Bennett/Oxfam

Jakudu in Nyamini Camp.

the SPLA to take the cattle.

I had the small children — I was running ahead with the other children — I had one on my back and I was carrying the other one and so the cattle were taken — I don't know where they are gone.

I stayed on there, but was alone all the time. I would collect green vegetables from the bush and make it for food, but as soon as the food was ready the SPLA would come and they would like to eat that.

When I escaped into the bush, I was alone but for my three children. On the way there were many people, so we came with other people. They said they were running away, too.

One of my children died on the way coming here. Now I am left with two; you can see them here. The child died because there was nothing to eat and there was no milk. It was the youngest that died.

It took six days on the way coming — when we got tired we would sit and rest or sleep in the place we were tired.

I am nine days here in Nyamini now. I had nothing with me when I arrived — I only came with my children. I have nothing.

I don't think I will go back home soon. Even if I go now, who is going to take care of me? I have nobody."

Jon Bennett

THE UNREPORTED WAR

BONA MALWAL

Bona Malwal graduated with a degree in economics and a diploma in mass media from universities in the United States. In 1965, he established the *Vigilant* newspaper in Khartoum. Three years later, he became a Member of Parliament. He was one of the founders of the Southern Front Party of southern Sudan and its first Secretary-General. From 1972-78, Bona Malwal was Minister for Culture and Information. From 1980-81, he served as Minister of Finance and Economic Planning of southern Sudan. He is currently editor-in-chief of *The Sudan Times*. He gives his views about the press in a question and answer interview. He starts by saying ...

Relations between the press and the government are touchy, even under the latest fledgling democracy. As with any government elsewhere in the world, the present one of Sadiq El Mahdi would like to manage the news and otherwise control the press. Efforts are under way to introduce a press law and there is a fear among journalists that the government will use a new law to manage the news and thus succeed in muzzling the media.

At present though, and this is to the government's credit, the government has so far confined itself to mere verbal assaults on the media. There has, on the whole, been free and unhindered reporting by the press except for one or two instances where journalists have been arrested.

Reporting on the civil war is a different matter entirely. There has been, in general, biased reporting of the situation in the civil war by the northern Arabic press. This is because that press is owned, managed and controlled by northerners and Muslims who mainly feel threatened by the south.

The Arabic press has sought to portray the SPLA-led rebellion as one of a foreign-dominated lawless group that has no real objectives. The government, meanwhile, largely manages the war news and at times deliberately misleads the public with regard to events in the war. The media, whether state-owned, partisan or independent, invariably echo the government's themes.

The intention is undoubtedly to keep the public in the north as ill-informed and as ignorant as possible about the real causes and facts of the war and the progress, or lack of it, being made in it. Emphasis is placed on pan-Arabic and Islamic goals to an extent that perpetuates Sudanese society's dichotomies.

It can be said that the Khartoum-based press has not critically covered the war and has made no effort to expose the full facts concerning its cost to the country and the draining away of resources. In that regard, the press has performed a disservice to the greater interests of the country.

The government, which has failed so badly in so many respects vis-a-vis Sudan's problems, has every reason to be pleased with the press on this point.

How many newspapers are there, and who owns them?

There are 25 to 30 newspapers. All, except two, are in Arabic. *The Sudan Times* is the only independent daily English-language newspaper in the country. There is another English weekly newspaper, otherwise the rest are in Arabic.

About 80% of the newspapers are owned by the Muslim Brothers movement, either directly as a party organ, or financed with the aim of projecting them to the public as being independent. Officially, the Muslim Brothers own only one newspaper, *El Rayah*, which is their official organ. But everybody in the country knows that they own the other newspapers, even though these are presented as being independent.

The Umma party has two or three papers. It has at least three other papers which are known to be affiliated, but Umma calls them independent newspapers. The DUP party also has two or three papers. Apart from these, there are two leading Arabic newspapers which are recognised as being independent.

All the newspapers are in Khartoum. There is no provincial newspaper in the Sudan.

In addition to the private sector, the government publishes a daily newspaper in English, about four weekly newspapers in Arabic and a weekly magazine.

The biggest newspaper is the Arabic *El Ayyam*, with about 50,000 copies a day. The smallest circulation among the newspapers is about 5,000.

On average, I would say that between 300,000 to 400,000 newspapers are sold each day. A readership of that size in a country like the Sudan means the media has extensive influence: hence the government's concern with what newspapers say.

Most party papers are read mainly by party supporters, but there is also a very wide independent readership. This worries the government; it knows its supporters will not be persuaded to the point of view of other parties, but it fears that the independent newspapers are influencing people across party lines, including members of its own party.

What about radio and television?

They are both state-owned. TV, I think, does not have as much impact as radio. But TV has a much more loyal audience than radio because it is able to provide greater entertainment, especially with films which come from Egypt and other parts of the the Arab world and which are liked by many of the northern Sudan population.

TV should by now have been widely spread because there are at least 18 relay stations all over the country; but TV does not extend much beyond the confines of Khartoum because of the degeneration in public services. Electricity is not available in many towns, so all you see of TV there are the antennae. But it has an impact in Khartoum and the surrounding areas and in the Gazira, which still has a semblance of good services.

Radio has wider coverage, but its reception is limited to a radius of about 200 kilometres (125 miles) around Khartoum, although at

A drawing by Safi Obale from Angutua primary school.

certain times of the night it can be heard in most parts of the country.

I do not know what its impact on the public is because, given the problems the country faces and given the untrue explanations the government offers, many people are mistrustful of what they get from the government media, especially radio and TV. The public sees radio and TV basically as machines for propaganda.

Can you speak about the coverage of the war which that range of media provides?

In most of the media, there is no coverage of the war to speak of. The media only waits to put out what the government forces say are their successes. Sometimes, some of the independent newspapers — like *The Sudan Times* — use reports which have been published elsewhere in the world, and these can upset the government.

But basically there is a silence, a conspiracy, in the Sudanese media in the sense that they don't publish any independent information and they will never say what damage is being done to the country by the guerilla army or the rebellion.

Why do the independent papers not attempt to provide some alternative?

No matter how independent they are, these are overwhelmingly northern Sudanese newspapers and northern Sudan is a very conformist society. But there are also difficulties of reporting: we cannot minimise those. If a newspaper wants to go to the south and report on the war it cannot go independently but has to go as part of the army, and as part of the army it will only report on the army's side of events. It cannot report on the other side.

What would happen if an independent newspaper tried to provide coverage from the other side? Would there be constraints on publication?

I don't think there would be constraints. If there is a paper actually willing to send reporters to the other side I believe it could publish the reports. But I don't think there is a newspaper in Khartoum which is willing to do that yet.

What you're saying implies that there is no real need for any formal constraints on the media because the informal constraints embedded in society are all that are needed?

Absolutely. And of course the constraints the government is looking for would not be constraints for the Arabic media because they are already constrained in that they feel they are part of the war, on the government's side. They even go beyond the government in their advocacy of the war.

What the government wants to go for are perhaps the very limited English-language newspapers, which are neither northern Sudanese owned or northern Sudanese run and which try to reflect what the other side stands for and what the other side is doing. Because of this and because there has been some restricted but very effective coverage of those events by this very small number of newspapers, any constraints would fall on them.

What sort of constraints?

Before the government came to think of legal constraints, it first tried a series of measures which it thought might work. One of these was to try to project those who do not go along with the government's view as being fifth columnists. I recently wrote an article to show it is a silly notion because a fifth column is an enemy from within who supports an enemy from without; in the civil war I don't think you can call anyone an enemy from without. You might say there are enemies within, but you can't call them fifth columnists.

But the government did, anyway, try to project and condemn as fifth columnists individuals who said that those who stand on the other side have grounds for doing so, and that if you don't answer those grounds you cannot expect to end the war. This did not work. It did not dissuade those people from continuing to take the stance they did.

So the government had to look for other means with which to constrain the media. One of these means was to refuse to provide newsprint in the traditional way whereby the government allocates foreign exchange for newsprint to be imported. Instead, the government simply said that there were no funds for this and newspapers had to find their own way of bringing in newsprint. If they had the means the government would have no objection.

When was this?

Last year, in 1987. It was clear that the government knew that some members of the media had better resources than others and that they could bring in newsprint and would therefore monopolise public opinion in the country. So it became an important constraint on the media to say: there's no newsprint available, and if you cannot provide your own, you perish.

Right up to now the government does not provide facilities for getting newsprint. But a lot of government-supported agencies, a lot of government party papers have in one way or another managed to bring newsprint into the country. They sell it at prohibitive prices. The idea, of course, is that if fledgling newspapers buy it they will use up their resources and die.

However, most papers haven't died. Perhaps the government is surprised by this and so now it wants to bring in legal constraints to liquidate newspapers.

At what stage is this?

It is still at the talking stage. No legislation has been put forward.

Within the limited coverage of the war, is there any attempt to indicate longer-term development costs?

Nothing, nothing at all. People are not being rational and are not trying to count the cost to them and to their country. The war is being treated as if it were a challenge to the northern ideology, to Islamic and Arab existence in the Sudan. When people look at the war in that way, costs are not important.

Until recently, though, the fighting was effectively limited to the South. Now that is beginning to change and the spillover — in terms of displaced people — is beginning to affect the rest of the country. Is that being reported and is it affecting public opinion about the war?

A tremendous number of people have come to northern Sudan from the war-torn southern Sudan. If the government of the northern community were to regard these people as Sudanese citizens of the same country and as people for whom they must care, the impact on the rest of the country would have been stunning. But these people are not seen like that. These are wretched, poor, hungry people who live on the outskirts of Khartoum and are viewed by the northern Sudanese as different from them. The plight of these people doesn't bother them. If it did, the northern community would organise relief assistance.

The feeling that these are sub-humans results in actions like the one we reported last year and which we are accused of exploiting for propaganda: the massacre at Diein in March 1987 in which more than 1,000 Dinka people were set on fire in a railway station while government forces watched.

This could not happen in a country which regarded itself as one and which regarded its people as one people.

So the southern Sudanese who have come to the north are for the large part refugees in a foreign country and refugees whom nobody wants to look after. The Sudan Government is doing nothing. The northern community is doing nothing. It is only the foreign community and the relief agencies which are trying to do something and even then hurdles are placed in the way of the relief agencies trying to help these people.

What press coverage has there been of the refugee situation around Khartoum?

Not as much as I suspect there could be. I am speaking of events such as 7,000 people arriving at the railway station. Nobody takes care of them, and they starve. Eventually they melt into the society, leaving seven dead bodies behind. This happened a few months ago. Only my newspaper reported it.

But there is one important impact which has to be noted. It occurs in rural western Sudan: it is through there that the southerners enter northern Sudan.

It has caused some irritation. The western Sudan community is very poor; it has a limited infrastructure or none at all. It is therefore sharing non-existent facilities with the large numbers of southerners who are coming in.

Has there been any press reporting of the impact of the war on the economy of western Sudan?

Yes, but again not as much as it should be.

There is also a change in the northern Sudanese view of the war. When Nimeiri was in power and the war started people thought it was a good thing that the south was not well-treated, that its autonomy was abrogated and that Nimeiri imposed Sharia on non-Muslims.

Northerners supported the war. But as soon as Nimeiri was overthrown, people in northern Sudan thought: that's it, democracy has come. They now wanted the south to end the war and be run in the same democratic way as they believed the rest of the country would be under Sadiq El Mahdi. They said there was an elected government which was willing to find a solution.

The south did not, however, stop fighting, and so there was a period, in 1986 and 1987, when many people said the south really did not want peace.

And now, in the same way, some northerners are beginning to understand that the so-called elected government has not come to find a solution, but to rule the country — perhaps in a worse way than Nimeiri.

So northern opinion is beginning to shift, to say maybe the southerners were right; if they had come, what would they have got? If they can't get it now while they are holding their guns, would they have got anything if they had come without being offered something?

THE AGONY OF THE FAMILY

KOSTI MANIBE

Kosti Manibe is Deputy General Secretary of the Sudan Council of Churches.

Since 1983, a gruelling civil war, fought in the most spirited fashion by the Sudan Government Army on the one side and the Sudan People's Liberation Army (SPLA) on the other, has raged in south Sudan. The war shows no sign of abating. The two main combatants have been joined by an array of auxiliary forces no less spirited in their zeal, although much less organised and much less disciplined.

Caught inbetween these opposing armies are about 6 million people, some 90% of whom live in the rural countryside. For this population, life is further complicated and made difficult at every turn by the roving bands of armed robbers, crooks and other soldiers of fortune who have seen an opportunity to exploit. Often masquerading as SPLA soldiers, thus securing the submission of their victims, these soldiers of fortune loot, plunder, even old scores with their enemies and former rivals, and hope, with some luck, to get rich in the process.

War, armed banditry and the social upheaval which has come in their wake, are having traumatic effects on individual members of society; on families and on whole communities. Thousands of people have seen family members, relatives and friends killed before their eyes. Some of these people have suffered instant death from gunfire or have been blown into shreds by landmines or anti-personnel mines.

Others have gone through more agonising ordeals — slow death through torture; or being gassed to death; or death through the inexperienced hands of small children who have not yet mastered the art of handling the spear but who are forced to do the job by a superior force, so as to make death a slow and painful experience for the victims.

People who have escaped a similar fate and those who have witnessed such incidents remain traumatised long afterwards. The psychological effect on them must be profound, to say the least. There are thousands of such people around, all with horrid stories of their experiences. Psychological trauma arising from witnessing such horrific scenes must have its greatest effect on children, however, with dire consequences for the future.

There are many thousands of such children who have miraculously escaped from death although subjected to indiscriminate hails of gunfire. Many more thousands of children have borne witness to the cruel torture and murder of parents or guardians. Many of these children cannot go to bed alone in a room without the reassuring presence of an adult near them. Others have developed a morbid fear of anybody in army or police uniform. Yet others spend their time playing battle-games between the SPLA and the government army.

While the effect of the war on individuals has been traumatic, the effect on society as a whole and on basic social institutions has been severe.

Breakdown of extended family

The extended African family is a well-documented social institution and does not need an exhaustive sociological definition here. For the purpose of this chapter we will use the concept of the homestead, the household and the extended family interchangeably.

In south Sudan it is not uncommon to find in a family unit — organised as a household or the homestead — parents, sons, unmarried daughters, grandparents, grandchildren, cousins, nieces and other relatives all living together. In an urban setting, the extended family unit live under the same roof.

Who lives in a particular household/homestead and the size of that family unit depends on factors such as the closeness of the kinship relationship, capacity of the individual household heads, the social standing of the key members of the family unit, economic resources under the control of the unit and the internal composition of other related family units within the kinship group.

What happens in one family unit may affect the composition of other family units as members move into it or out of it. The death of an only child could mean other kinsmen stepping in and giving their own children to be raised as part of the bereaved family unit.

Generally speaking, the higher the social standing of the household head, the larger the size of the extended family unit; the more economic resources under the control of a family unit, the larger its size. All members of the various nationalities in south Sudan are organised into households and homesteads in one of these extended family units.

To date, well over 80% of the land area of southern Sudan has been affected by the civil war. The entire population of some 6 million people has been affected directly or indirectly.

Although statistics are not available and figures passed around are suspect, a conservative estimate of the number of people displaced at one time or another can be put at 3 million. Of these, roughly 1 million have totally migrated from their normal place of residence in the rural countryside and sought refuge in main towns in the south such as Juba, Wau and Malakal.

But the majority of the new rural migrants who have not re-established themselves in other rural locations have gone to northern Sudan, where ostensibly, peace, security and a life of dignity lies in wait, in the "caring" hand of the government.

Given the large numbers involved and the extended family system, it is no exaggeration to say that every family unit in south Sudan has been affected along the way.

Membership of the extended family confers rights and privileges to be enjoyed, but also carries with it obligations and responsibilities which must be fulfilled. The hospitality rendered, the accommodation provided, the feeding received, the assistance when in distress, all have to be reciprocated — not necessarily in

"Where the shadow of immediate danger does not loom large in the camps, the family unit has held firmly together, sharing the little that is available, supporting one another and comforting those in pain."

kind but in some form. Reciprocation should not only be made to the person or the family which has rendered the support, but to the other members of the extended family and kinship group as well.

How then does this system of social security and mutual support respond to the strain and stress of war and social upheaval?

In some respects, the extended family system has performed surprisingly well. In urban centres like Juba, Wau, Malakal and Khartoum, the number of people living in the house of an average southerner ranges from 15 to 30. It is not uncommon to find households of 40 to 50 people. Many heads of these sprawling urban households do not even know the total number of people living in their houses. Indeed some wonder how the people, including themselves, manage to keep alive on the income they earn.

The camp situation, where the displaced have congregated in large numbers — anything from 200 to 20,000 — is another setting in which the extended family system and communal responsibilities have fared well. Where the shadow of immediate danger does not loom large, the family unit has held firmly together, sharing the little that is available, supporting one another and comforting those in pain.

A sense of community with shared responsibility for the welfare of one another, even among people who have not known each other before, has been evident. Those who have lost their dear ones in the camp have received consolation and support from other camp residents. Assistance to meet burial and funeral rites, sometimes in the form of small cash contributions from people who are equally in need of the money, are part of their expression of solidarity.

Respect for one's elders, irrespective of whether they are from among one's kinsmen or not, which is an honoured African tradition, continues to be observed in the camps for the displaced. New communities are thus in the making being drawn, in some measure, on old patterns.

In other respects, the extended family and communal responsibilities have fared less well.

In the rural countryside, especially those areas where the contest for control of territory and for minds and souls still rages, security considerations have become the prime determinants of social behaviour. Couples with small and noisy little children have been pushed away and forced to set up their homestead a considerable distance from the other members of the extended family and community.

Likewise, people who keep livestock in communities where animal husbandry is not a common practice, have been forced to live apart from the others. Domestic animals are a handy source of food to the combatants of this war and are attractive items to soldiers of fortune out to seek wealth.

Indeed, security considerations have become so basic in some rural areas that a discernible pattern of movement towards the nuclear family in setting up households and homesteads is emerging.

The effect of security is seen in a practice evolved to cope with the behaviour of a domestic animal — the cock. A contraption made of a thin rubber band has been devised and is put round the neck of a cock to prevent it from crowing loudly. The sight of cocks

Michel Croce-Spinelli/Gamma

Rebel fighters harassing villagers.

wearing these contraptions might be amusing but the security concerns of the people are real.

Ominous signs of increasing deviance in social behaviour are emerging among rural folk with strong community bonds and strict codes of social conduct but who have been exposed to camp conditions. The incidence of stealing is reported to have vastly increased. The machinery of the social sanction which keeps such behaviour in check in the traditional setting is missing in the new environment and new constraints have not been devised as yet.

Impact of looting

Looting is a feature of most wars and this one is no exception. Some of the effects on the population and on the economy have been devastating. Given the meagre resources of the country, the future costs of looting on social and economic development of the area could be phenomenal. In some respects, the damage wrought by looting might be irreversible and will mean fundamental changes in the lifestyle of some people.

Animals play a pivotal role in the social and economic life of

Caroline Penn/Reflex

Government troops searching homes in Wau.

pastoral societies, including many of the south Sudanese affected by the war. Animals represent more than the mark of wealth and serve purposes other than as instruments in ordering social relationships: they are the food security of last resort.

It is feared, with reason, that the Shilluk of Upper Nile may have lost all their cattle as a result of looting. In northern Bahr el Ghazal — in the Gogrial and Aweil areas — the local population have lost large herds of cattle because of looting. Some of the Dinka cattle have appeared in markets as far north as Khartoum. Looting of livestock has affected other areas as well, though to a lesser extent.

Wholesale loss of animals — cattle — in parts of northern Bahr el Ghazal has resulted in starvation on a scale whose exact magnitude remains unknown to date. Migration out of the area, partly as a result of this loss, has swollen the population of towns in the northern Sudan and raised eyebrows about its potential political significance.

The number of animals looted remains unknown. It could easily be as high as the number of the displaced themselves.

Whereas some of the stolen animals have merely changed hands and could still be counted as part of the local economy, some have been eaten while others have been driven off to distant markets. Besides, therefore, loss of food security, the people who have migrated "temporarily" from their home areas might not be able to go back home and resume their old lifestyle. The means are not there anymore. And to restore this lifestyle would involve organising a massive programme of restocking, involving hundreds of thousands of animals.

Among farming communities, looting of food has lowered the threshold of the anti-hunger security of subsistence farmers. Food reserve levels have become drastically reduced. The worst impact of looting in this regard might be on seed stocks — which are being consumed. There is danger of the permanent loss of good crops which have been carefully selected and tested over the centuries, thus increasing even more the vulnerability to famine of the people in some marginal areas of food production.

Nor have fixed assets escaped being looted. The zinc roofs of public institutions like schools, dispensaries, health centres and other public and private buildings have been removed and carried off. Machinery, equipment and vehicles have also been stolen in many parts of south Sudan. Some have appeared in markets in urban centres of the south; but most have been taken to Khartoum and other parts of northern Sudan by their new "owners". To rehabilitate these structures and facilities when the war finally ends will cost huge sums of money.

Rural/urban exodus

Rural to rural displacement has affected most rural folk, especially in borderline areas where the battle for control between the combatants has not been conclusively settled. This displacement entails no fundamental changes in the lifestyle of the affected population other than having to move their homesteads a few kilometres, or a few tens of kilometres.

However, it is the phenomenon of rural/urban migration which has entailed basic changes in lifestyle.

Between 1 to 1.2 million people from the rural countryside have migrated to urban centres. The majority — about 800,000 — have

Caroline Penn/Reflex

Building a new home in a camp outside Wau.

migrated to urban centres in northern Sudan, while the rest are scattered between Juba, Wau, Malakal and a host of other smaller towns in southern Sudan.

Driven off by war, these rural migrants have gone to urban centres in search of peace and security. They have made the tedious and arduous journey in the belief that the mighty and welcoming hand of the government waits to receive them. More often than not, the displaced receive a rude shock on arrival at their new destinations. Finding themselves unwelcome and uncared for, those lucky enough to have members of their extended family or other kinsmen around, fall back on the security of age-old institutions — the extended family, marriage ties, etc.

The rural displaced who have sought refuge in urban centres regard themselves as temporary residents, ready to go back to their homes the first day peace returns. But while the war lasts they have to earn a living and learn to cope with urban living. Back home, the lifestyle they were used to might be changing irreversibly.

Can they ever make it back to the rural countryside when peace finally arrives, assuming they will still be alive?

The rural to urban migration, which is more or less on the pattern of migrations elsewhere, is a known phenomenon. The more interesting phenomenon, of urban to rural migration, has passed unnoticed. But it exists. The basic considerations have not been so much security as lack of food. The rural displaced have moved into Malakal and Wau while the town residents of these same urban centres have moved out into the rural countryside. From a host of other smaller towns significant numbers of people have left the urban centres for the security of the rural countryside.

Some of the town residents who have fled into the rural countryside are government officials. Others have skills in agriculture, extension work, community development and health care. It would be interesting to see how they apply these skills and knowledge to the task of rural development and provision of services where they now live. It might be even more interesting to see what insights they take back should they choose to return to their former occupations after the war ends.

The cost of labour

Thousands of displaced people in urban areas and in camps set up close to urban centres for security reasons, would ordinarily be associated with low rates of pay. Large numbers of them are hunting for jobs — while many job-openings are closing down because of the downturn in economic activity.

Business life, on the other hand, has responded more rationally to the present situation: most business activities have closed down. Petty rural businesses have suffered the greatest. Most have lost their entire capital. Others lack the opportunity to move into new business lines and have closed their doors; yet others are too weary to take risks while the war continues.

Risk-taking is virtually inseparable from business activities. The greater the risk, the more the profit. This business wisdom distilled over the centuries is being used to the letter in the south Sudan of today by a small number of businessmen and a handful of adventurers. The most lucrative line of business is in the food trade.

Some businessmen risk their lives and their capital, spending weeks at a time travelling in army convoys to ply their trade. Those who do arrive at the other end of the journey make huge profits commensurate with the risks involved.

Truck-owners are still prepared to chance having their vehicles blown up by landmines and hire them out to those who wish to make use of them. Of course, the hire charges are sky-high. Petty traders from the rural areas under the control of the SPLA have defied the wrath of both the SPLA and the security personnel of the government (who often accuse them of being spies) and continue to trade between the countryside and urban centres. They exchange the goods of one area for the produce of the other. With or without the permission of the powers that be, this trade continues.

The war has brought about a situation of very high risks for business but it has also provided unprecedented opportunities. Those who take the risks and survive the dangerous roads, and those who negotiate their way through the lines of the various armies, rake up huge profits. Such levels of profit continue to inspire daredevils to defy all odds in their race to make money.

While the majority of the people try to eke out a living under these difficult conditions, losing their purchasing power by the day as rampant inflation wreaks havoc, a small number of people are mining wealth at an amazing rate. Thus millions are becoming more and more impoverished while a small number are rapidly climbing the ladder on their way to become millionaires.

SOUTHERN KORDOFAN: On the day this photograph was taken in June 1988, about 20,000 displaced people had made their way out of northern Bahr El Ghazal to the small garrison town of Abyei in southern Kordofan. Every two weeks, the Catholic mission was distributing foodgrain: on this day, an estimated 7,000 women came for food.

Later in the day, the government hastily arranged a feeding programme for the children and adults. Those who came for this second distribution were severely malnourished; many appeared to be walking skeletons.

A constant stream of people was moving on from Abyei further into south Kordofan, to what they hoped would be comparative safety. But that safety was far from certain: during the previous year's rainy season, the SPLA made indiscriminate attacks in the region and the government's two MIG planes stationed at El Obeid made bombing raids on known SPLA positions.

After the rains, the army cleared three villages around Um Darein where they suspected villagers had fed the SPLA; the militia then burnt down houses and made off with livestock and crops.

THE FOUR ENEMIES

MARCELLO LADO JADA

Assistant Director for Co-ordination and Field Management, Equatoria region, Juba

The civilian population in south Sudan see four enemies, all of them deadly: government troops, the Sudan People's Liberation Army (SPLA), the tribal militias, and famine. And they are defenceless against any of these. This is the state of affairs in every corner of the south today.

Killing and looting are prominent. Civilian casualties have far outnumbered those among the armed forces. A veritable genocide is being perpetrated.

Human life is precious and its loss is unacceptable, whether in mid-air or on the ground, for whatever reason. Hundreds of people are dying daily in the south and the international press is paying little attention, to say the least. Even the most internationally famous professors of anthropology who have studied and written about the Dinkas, Nuer, Azande and others, seem to have forgotten that the people with whom they once sat around the fire are being exterminated.

In all corners of the south, people are fleeing for safety, a journey some of them do not complete.

About 1 million people are in Khartoum and western Sudan, and in Darfur and Kordofan provinces after fleeing from the south. Hundreds of thousands of displaced people cling to camps on the edges of towns in the south. Similar numbers are found across the borders in Ethiopia and Uganda.

Damage to the culture

Culture may be defined as the complex whole that makes one society different from the other. African society is strongly communal in nature and much is done within the framework of interdependence, common efforts and support of one another. But in the present war, the communal element of human co-existence has been lost. The responsibility of one member of the society towards others is no longer a practice. The security of the society is therefore at stake.

The breakdown of culture is also seen in the fate of oral literature which passes tradition by word of mouth. Like other African societies, tribes and people in southern Sudan share a rich heritage of stories, proverbs, poems, songs and riddles. It is a common phenomenon in an African society that in the evening a family sits around the fire to listen to the elderly recalling their ancestral wisdom and bravery and heroes. It is a reflection of self-confidence inherited from their traditions. This creates in the youth of the society a feeling of unity, security and assurance that they are part and parcel of their people and are linked with the past.

Alas! this can no longer happen in any corner of the south where people are living in tents or on open ground and where the concern for survival and security occupies the entire mind of people, old or young.

Religion has also suffered. African religion offers a link through ancestral spirits to the supernatural being. Religion, rooted in the cultural system, respects the norms and values of society and provides an understanding of the supernatural forces.

The war has wrecked the value system in our society, and many people are questioning the power of God. This kind of development can make society degenerate into a fatalistic stance, and hence slavery and exploitation can regenerate.

Erosion of morality

A major concern of every southerner is the serious consequences of a breakdown of moral values resulting from insecurity and lack of opportunities for education and development. Among the indicators of the crisis are the destruction of family bonds, the loss of the sense of the value and dignity of human life, and the growing mentality of violence. These are examples ...

In May 1987, in Maridi, a police car carrying seven or eight policemen was destroyed by a landmine, presumably planted by the SPLA. When the news was heard, relatives of the dead police went on the rampage, burning huts, beating and killing any Dinka passing their way. They used arrows, sticks and pangas (machetes), and killed three unarmed Dinkas. Survivors took refuge inside Maridi Catholic Church.

In July 1987, 30 displaced people, including women and children, were gunned down at Nesitu, just 15 miles from Juba on the Torit road, apparently by SPLA rebels. Several others were seriously injured and had to be admitted to Juba Teaching Hospital; they told how the rebels, without provocation, bombarded the camp for half an hour with rocket-propelled guns and handgrenades.

They said that the 11 policemen guarding the camp took to their heels without responding to the shootings; when the rebels found that there was no response, they rampaged into the camp killing, looting and destroying tents. They said that the SPLA told them they were killing them to show the government that the situation was "alarming". All the victims had fled their homes three months earlier, after another attack by the rebels.

Is it logical for a so-called liberation movement like the SPLA to kill the very oppressed people they claim to fight for? Right-thinking Sudanese will agree that killing of these unarmed persons amounts to murder and is a terrorist act which should be strongly condemned.

But the SPLA should not be singled out for condemnation alone. In Wau, on 11 and 12 August 1987, it was reported, the army attacked three residential quarters and killed at least 600 people, most of whom were women and children. In April 1988, in Juba's residential area of Muniki, the army went on the rampage, burning 40 houses. Similar incidents happened at Atalabara market in Juba town, the dancing hall and Equatoria Inn.

In one of the incidents in Juba, in March 1988, armed soldiers

Lologo camp was established in December 1986, two miles outside Juba. By June 1987, there were 5,000 displaced people resettled at the site; a year later, the camp had become an entire new village with 20,000 displaced resettled there.

from one of the barracks tortured civilians and burnt down huts and businesses belonging to southerners at Rujal Mafi market. The following morning, in reaction to this, violence erupted between residents and northern traders in the market. Three traders were beaten to death.

The displaced people

At the time of writing in July 1988, there are 12 camps for the displaced around Juba, providing refuge for more than 80,000 people. The camps are around the town, most within a few miles' radius. The numbers of the displaced grew rapidly in the first half of 1988, with agencies distributing 100,000 tonnes of relief food a month in Juba town alone.

Several thousand others who refuse to live in the camps live with their relatives in town. But life in Juba town has become extremely difficult and they are no better off than those in the camps.

The town of Yei has 37,000 displaced people. Here too, numbers have grown rapidly: at the start of 1988 there were only 4,000. All are in the town, not in camps, for fear of attack. Wau has 20,000 displaced people, but relief food has not been getting through and people have been leaving the town. Many more displaced people are in other parts of the south, some of them in an inhuman state of existence.

Once people arrive in camps, they receive some support in the form of food and clothing. Most of the residents of the camps around Juba have an income, whether from growing vegetables, making charcoal, cutting grass, or blacksmithing. However, the income is very limited and, with the high price of grain, insufficient to feed a family. In any event, grain has not been arriving in Juba in sufficient quantities to satisfy the needs even of the salaried townspeople, so there is little for the displaced people.

The relief effort became entirely Sudanese in 1988. The expatriates left and it turned into a programme run by Sudanese staff, helping their own displaced. But the relief agencies have been increasingly forced to depend on the military as the number of the displaced has grown.

Food aid coming to southern Sudan arrives first in Juba, either by air from Nairobi or by road through Uganda. The agencies are not permitted to deliver their food to other towns without a military escort, apart from one or two specified exceptions. Many people feel that the government troops are preventing food from leaving army-garrisoned towns in a bid to weaken rebel control over the southern countryside.

The army will never make a trip only to accompany relief supplies. So the agencies have to stay in touch with army personnel to learn when a convoy is leaving — in the hope that they can add their lorries of food aid, even though military convoys are often attacked by rebels.

The Juba-Torit convoy

This is exactly what happened in mid-May 1988. Word began to spread in Juba that a military convoy would soon be going to Torit — normally a three-hour drive. No convoy had gone for six months. Deprived of food aid, 10 to 20 people, adults as well as children, were dying of starvation in Torit each day.

The relief agencies generally hire their lorries from private traders, at great expense: the Juba-Torit route is £S2,500 (US$625)

per tonne — in addition to the costs already incurred in buying the food and transporting it to Juba. So when the rumour got round, the agencies charged with supplying food to that part of the region rushed to hire transport and to load up their sacks of grain.

But like most Juba rumours, it was premature; the lorries had to be unloaded and then loaded again twice more before they finally set off one Sunday morning.

There were more than 50 vehicles in the convoy: 18 were relief lorries carrying 150 tonnes of food; the others were armoured personnel vans and lorries, as well as minesweepers — large bulldozers flailing long chains in an effort to explode any mines in the road ahead.

The convoy travelled at walking pace. When it hit the first landmine, the commander wanted to turn back, and was replaced. It ran into a heavy attack at Ngangalla: the SPLA had laid mines in the road and mounted an ambush when the convoy stopped.

The three-hour journey took four weeks.

When the convoy finally arrived in Torit on 1 July, 27 people had been killed, five of them civilians. Only 12 of the 18 relief lorries completed the journey: two were burnt in the ambush and four broke down.

The food the convoy delivered probably helped Torit survive for another two months. But the townspeople knew that they would starve again, sooner or later.

This explains why, despite the risks, whenever a military convoy leaves Torit for Juba, as many people as possible try to travel with it. One convoy of 80 army vehicles left Torit in March 1988, with 3,000 to 4,000 civilians walking alongside or piled on to the vehicles. Twenty people were killed along the road by anti-personnel mines and when the convoy arrived at Lirya, the army arranged for a helicopter to fly the wounded for the rest of the journey. As the helicopter took off, about 30 other people who had been walking with the convoy tried to get on board, clinging to the outside of the aircraft. As the pilot struggled for height, the helicopter overturned and crashed: 40 people died.

Many problems exist for people even when they manage to get to the camps. Towards the end of February 1988, a landmine blew up an army lorry on the road just north of the Boatyard camp outside Juba. Government troops harassed the displaced people in the camp, presumably believing them to have knowledge of the mine-laying: soldiers fired shots into the air and took tools such as pangas and axes. Also, the military no longer allowed people to go into the bush, preventing the displaced from carrying out their usual work of collecting poles, grass, firewood and charcoal for sale.

Two weeks after this, the rebels attacked Gumbo and, while retreating, placed anti-personnel mines in and around the same Boatyard settlement, killing eight of the displaced civilians. The entire population — about 7,000 people — immediately evacuated the area. The government accepted that the site was no longer secure for settlement.

The SPLA are using these anti-personnel landmines in increasing quantities, in place of direct hand-to-hand combat. They place mines in roads to blow up vehicles, but also under fruit trees and in village water-holes. The victims are generally not military people, but defenceless southern civilians. In mid-June 1988, one such mine exploded when villagers were drawing water from their water-hole in Jebel Lado, 25 miles north of Juba. Four people were killed and another seven victims had to be taken to Juba hospital, some with their legs blown off.

The civilian population find themselves helpless in the middle of the conflict. The military do not trust the displaced people in the settlements, suspecting them of collaboration with the rebels. The rebels find the settlements an obstacle in their attacks on targets in the area. Many settlements live in fear of night attacks by the rebels. Some of the villagers in the Rejaf area south west of Juba have moved onto nearby small islands in the river for security. Few people remain in the Rejaf villages during the night, preferring to sleep in Juba or by the riverside where they can hide in the thick bush.

Social breakdown

Such is the life of southerners behind the front lines of the two warring armies — particularly those living in the camps. Why do the Sudanese Government and the SPLA appear to be so insensitive to the immense suffering of the people? Children are physically and mentally impaired, their future is doomed and the hope for effective contribution to the development of the south is lost.

Some of these people once owned lands, houses and fields and cattle. They had homes which they could call their own. Now, here they are, homeless and empty-handed. Still more painful as an African is the breakdown in the family system. Families are broken up. Some people do not know where the other members of their families are. They do not know whether they are alive or dead. These people are fleeing from the brutal activities of government militia and the SPLA. They flee because of the killing of innocent people and the widespread confiscation of their properties by armed men.

When the displaced arrive in Juba, they first go to a relative in the town. Everybody has a social obligation to look after a relative. But the relief agencies say that no-one will get food aid in Juba unless registered in a camp: there is no other way to organise the food distribution, they say. Therefore, if you live in Juba and your elderly parents arrive, fleeing from the fighting in the bush, you are forced to say to them: go to the camp.

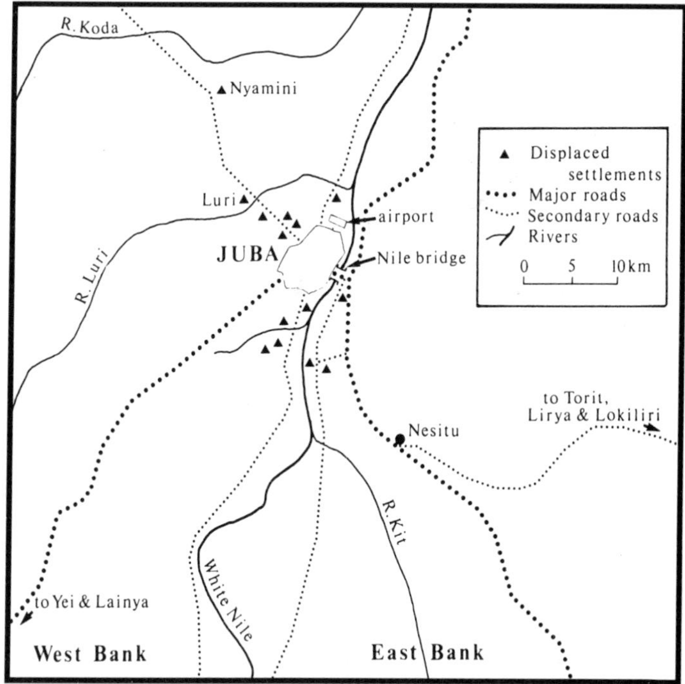

The procedure for food distribution seems to be necessary, but it means that traditional social responsibility is reduced. Many people in Juba feel that it is beginning to have an impact on family ties.

We also see the same thing among the young, with indications of a loss of social identity. One secondary school teacher in Juba tells of asking a class of 16-year-olds to write about the history of their clan. Almost none of the 36 young people could do so. Many did not even know the names of their grandparents, or of the village their clan came from. Not a single one could describe traditional social ceremonies.

The war has struck not only the lives of individual southerners, but also the very fabric of their society and tribal traditions. This is a sad moment for a southerner. Southern Sudan is far behind the north in socio-economic development; but now, instead of building, even more destruction is taking place.

Huge migrations

After the end of the 1955-1972 civil strife, the southern population stabilised, with only a few people migrating to major towns like Juba, Wau and Malakal. The massive south-north migration of the late-1950s and early-1960s ceased, and the south experienced north-south migration.

The present war, however, has resulted in an unprecedented migration in all directions. Internally, more than 250,000 have migrated to the north. Between February and May 1988 alone, 100,000 left Bahr el Ghazal to seek refuge in northern Sudan. This trend is getting worse as the war continues to ravage the region.

Externally, a similar trend of migration is taking place. During February and May 1988, 400,000 displaced people left Bahr el Ghazal for refuge in Ethiopia. Earlier, even greater numbers had crossed the border into Ethiopia from Upper Nile region and Bahr el Ghazal.

A large number of Sudanese refugees are also in Uganda. They have run away from both the SPLA and the army. And they equally fear the militias as dangerous forces who follow behind the army and the SPLA to complete what the others were unable to finish.

Too few jobs

Because many people are chasing few jobs in the south, pay is low. This is particularly common for houseboys and those working for shopkeepers or as dishwashers in restaurants.

Traders, on the other hand, say that one does not have to go to Saudi Arabia to become rich (in Sudan, Saudi Arabia is regarded as a guaranteed source for getting rich). Instead, the south is said to provide all such opportunities at this time: a particular commodity can at times cost twice as much in Juba as it does in Khartoum, and three times as much in Wau.

Business in the south is dominated by northern traders: about 95% are northerners. For years, since independence, they have transferred their money to the north. Southerners do not believe that businessmen from the north have contributed to the development of the south in any form.

Southerners who go into business struggle to survive against the northerners, and either remain as petty traders or fail completely. A survey of the non-formal sector of the economy in Juba in 1988 revealed that southerners engage in more than 200 smallscale businesses, including fishing, carpentry, foodselling, leathercraft and blacksmithing. Life has really become hard for most people in Juba. As one drives or walks across the town, one cannot miss seeing people selling all sorts of stuff — wheat flour, maize, milk, charcoal, firewood, grass or tea. Most of the sellers are women struggling to survive.

It is worse in other towns and villages in southern Sudan. If you look at the people in the war zones you see nothing but hunger and death written on their faces. This is where the businessmen know no morals. They exploit the people. A bag of dura (a variety of sorghum) in Wau in the early-1980s cost £S35 (US$8.75); by July 1988, it was reported to cost £S1,000 (US$250) or more. In Juba the price was £S400-500 (US$100-150).

The income levels of displaced people vary considerably. Most of them are farmers or pastoralists and do not have skills relevant to the towns. They go around searching for part-time work or odd jobs. Desperate, they are forced to take any job offered. Because of the unavailability of jobs, those who employ them offer any wage.

In Khartoum and other towns, the displaced people have been forced to do casual jobs like car-washing or housework. Lack of jobs and the erosion of traditional family discipline have combined to produce a generation which has nothing to lose.

A survey conducted in 1987 in camps for the displaced showed increasing income differentiation. In two camps, people receiving monthly incomes between £S200-300 (US$50-75) were 8% and 3.2% respectively. In the third camp, none of those interviewed had any monthly income.

Overall, about 40.4% of those interviewed had no monthly income; 39.3% had up to £S100 (US$25) a month, and 12.3% had up to £S200 (US$50) a month.

These striking differences in income reflect the gravity of the situation in the camps. Life in the camps is really hell.

By July 1988, more than 80,000 displaced people were in camps around Juba. Among them were people from villages about 25 miles away, on the road to Yei. Marcello Lado Jada spoke to them...

How many days did it take to walk here?
Because we are weak now and carrying children, bringing old women and men, and a few remaining belongings, it took one and a half days for the fastest of us, three days for the slowest.

What was the final thing that made you leave the village?
It was the SPLA. They took away everything we had, food, clothes, animals, and they beat us up. We had cultivated and some of us were about to weed.

How long has this kind of treatment been going on?
The SPLA have been coming into the area in small and big numbers for three years now. Once they arrive in the village they take everything from us. We tried not to leave the village, but as it kept happening, we decided to see what the government can do for us.

What about the neighbouring villages? Are these things happening to them?
Oh yes, this has been happening in all the villages around us, many people have died of hunger. The last thing we witnessed was the SPLA burning three lorries which came from Juba to our village to collect charcoal; some people were shot.

Have the old people ever experienced anything like this before in their lifetime?
Old people: The last war which we experienced was the Anya-Nya I war. But the Anya-Nya were good. Once they came to the village they asked for the Chief, they asked for food and the villagers gave it to them.
The SPLA are totally the opposite, they are so brutal, our experiences are very bad.
When they arrive in the village they rape young girls and women. They take away food, clothes and livestock by force. If anyone does not give what they want, he can be tied, stripped naked and beaten badly. It is this kind of treatment that made us leave the village.
Women: The SPLA are not friendly. As soon as they arrive in the village, everyone is scared. They like to take away women to have sex, both old women and very young girls — whatever age, they do not care. Our small boys of 12-15 are often beaten.

Have you lived in these villages for a long time?
Yes, it is our ancestral place. Our grandparents and great-grandparents lived there. It is painful to leave our villages just to live under a tree. Here we have nothing to put on, all the

clothes we had have been taken away, we have nothing to cover the children with, no blankets to cover with. We have some grain but not enough: you can see here how much we were given.
This is never a home.

WHY THEY FLED

MIKE WOOLDRIDGE

Mike Wooldridge is East Africa correspondent for the BBC, based in Nairobi.

Sudanese refugees started to arrive in western Ethiopia during the first few months of 1983, escaping from the renewed conflict. But numbers began to increase rapidly in 1988; by August, an estimated 300,000 had crossed the border ...

At Itang refugee camp in Ethiopia, the Rev Benjamin Terah, a priest from Juba, now acts as a liaison person between the United Nations High Commissioner for Refugees (UNHCR) and the refugee community. We talk in the therapeutic feeding centre as we look at near-silent rows of skeletal young men. He says they have come very long distances, some walking for up to three months.

Terah translates for a very thin boy who calls himself James John. He says he is 18, but looks no more than 13 or 14. He explains that he became thin from hunger before he left his home town, Mundri.

He ran away because of hunger as well as war. "The plants had dried up in the ground," he explains. He came with four members of his family and will go back to Sudan "when the war stops."

We go to a place at the camp entrance where new arrivals are assembled. There are perhaps 200 of them: men, women and children. With Terah interpreting, they say that they all came from an area north of Malakal: "We have to find friends and relatives who can help us. We have not been registered here yet."

"Fleeing", a drawing by James Buga, Adio.

The houses of some of them were burnt down before they left. They say that entire families were wiped out. To get to Itang, they walked for more than one and a half months. They estimate that a quarter of their number died en route. They are the first from their area to arrive here and say that others who were behind them may arrive or may have lost their lives.

They say that they have "no side" in the war. "We are only civilians who have been affected by the war."

Samuel Dak was director of local government and administration in Bahr el Ghazal region. Now he is chairman of the refugees' committee at Itang camp. "The governor of Bahr el Ghazal thought we were in opposition," he says. "I was marked. I went to the bush — I thought I might have been killed. I went for my own life, not to join the SPLA. My wife and small children came with me. We were 150 in our group. When we arrived here we were skeletons."

He claims that the policy of the Sudanese Government is to eliminate the educated and the male population to deprive the SPLA of manpower.

I ask how many more refugees he thinks will come. He claims that Arab militias take small girls as slaves and says people will continue coming to Ethiopia as long as Sadiq el Mahdi arms such people. He says some Dinka and Nuer people go to swampy areas within Sudan where they cannot be reached by the government forces. "As long as their cattle are with them they will try to survive," he says.

Dr Girma Makonnen shows me a very weak child. "This is a typical case of marasmus, protein deficiency. The chances of this child surviving are very poor. She has a very high chance of getting an infection."

Dr Koang Tut joins us. We find out that the girl's name is Nyanial Gac. She is 9 months old. Her mother says this is her second child. Her husband is dead. She and Nyanial came four months ago from Upper Nile region. The child has deteriorated at Itang: Dr Tut says she has less than 60% chance of survival. The child vomits when given food through her mouth; her stomach is unable to absorb the food.

Fugnido camp

At the Fugnido refugee camp, I talk to a family who have come from Bentiu in Bahr el Ghazal. One of them, Samira Nyatap, explains what happened: "We were chased away by government militias."

Was her own house attacked? "Yes. We don't know why. So many people were killed ... It took us two months and 22 days to get here. We ate leaves of the trees, occasionally an animal that had died. We had a small jerrycan of water. Many children died on the way."

The family say about 400 of them started out from Bentiu together; about 300 arrived in Ethiopia. Samira says she became separated from her husband when they first escaped; she doesn't know whether he is dead or alive. She lost two of her children on the way.

I talk to a man in his fifties with scars of bullet wounds, Yol Ngor from Aweil District. He says that the government militia attacked his village, killed his brother, his children and his cows. They took some women. They shot at him and then tried to kill him with a spear. He was unconscious for a time but managed to escape, although it was difficult to move on the journey. He depended on leaves for food.

A group of boys tell me that other boys were killed on the way. One says that his elder brother went to look for water in their village back in Sudan and did not come back. They tell how government

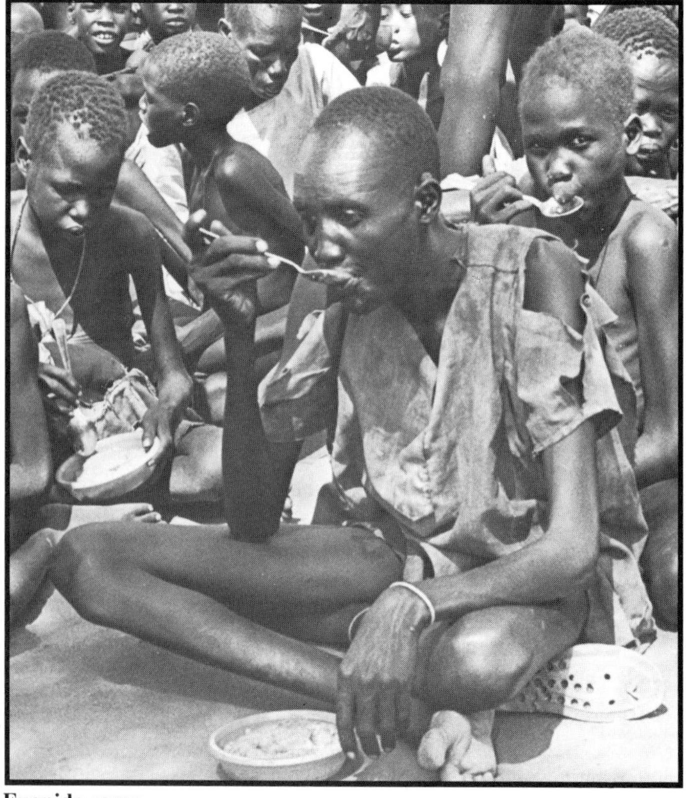

Camerapix

Fugnido camp

militias took womenfolk, burnt houses, stole food and cattle.

One boy has a very disfigured shoulder and neck. He explains that he was thrown into a burning house by militiamen.

Another family group tell me that they took two months to reach Fugnido camp from Pacong village, near Rumbek. "We had a lot of difficulties. There were so many swampy places — some of us got lost in the swamps and some of us lost our children that way. People were shooting at us from a helicopter and so we concealed ourselves. So many died on the way."

Why did you leave Rumbek? "Our houses and villages were set on fire by the government army. We were just looking for survival. No-one encouraged us to come. Either you escape or you die."

THE SPREADING CRISIS

Hilat Shook is one of the 23 communities of displaced people around the capital, Khartoum. Each community is ethnically distinct. In Hilat Shook the displaced are Nuer and Dinka from the Upper Nile region of southern Sudan.

Previously they were cattle-keeping people living in wide-open, thinly-populated country. As a result of the war, home for them became a crowded collection of cardboard "tukules" (huts) on a garbage dump on the edge of Khartoum. There was no running water, no electricity and no latrine facilities. A survey early in 1987 showed that a high proportion (34%) of households were headed by women; the prevalence of diarrhoea was put at 45% and only 7% of children had been immunised.

Alfred Logune Taban, a journalist with the magazine Sudanow, interviewed some of the people of Hilat Shook ...

John Juch Deng is 42 years old and was a farmer in his home district of Awiel, in Bahr el Ghazal region. Deng, a Dinka, fled in 1986 when the government-supported Arab militiamen invaded his area. He left behind 120 head of cattle and several acres of cultivated land.

Deng now makes £S170 (US$42.5) a month working as a watchman at the premises of the Sudanese Farmers' Union in Khartoum. "I used to make more than that in one market day back at home," he says.

Deng also has to provide for his two wives and seven children.

Ngak Bul Nyiking is a professional builder. He is 35 years old and fled from his home, in Mayom district in Upper Nile region, in 1983 when Anya-Nya II and the SPLA clashed in the area.

Nyiking does not understand English or Arabic, and cannot find work. Although he lost four brothers and his 120 head of cattle in the conflict, he says that he would rather be in the south than in Khartoum. He misses his people so much.

Solomon Maning Deng is 26. He used to be a petty trader in salt, dura and other essential commodities between his home of Pareng in Upper Nile region and Malakal. He left his home area when his 70 head of cattle were looted by Anya-Nya II. Now he is unemployed.

Deng, a Dinka, says he doesn't know what to do because trading has been his profession. But in Khartoum he cannot do that: nobody will give him the capital to start a business.

William Magok Bol, 23, is a teacher. He fled his home area of Gogrial in May 1986 to escape an attack made in the area by Marahelin (mobile) Arab militiamen. In order to live, Bol joined the National Islamic Front in Khartoum, and they found him a job as a watchman. His salary is £S280 ($US70) a month.

But Bol's job came at a price. He had to change from being a Christian to a Muslim and even had to take a Muslim name in place of William.

Bol has work, but he is far from happy. "From my small salary, I have to provide for several people at Hilat Shook who come from my home area," he says.

Besides, he finds that, unlike the south, there is virtually no social life in Khartoum. He says that the weather is uncomfortable, people who want to drink alcohol must do so in secret, the people are strange and there are few places to visit.

Nyton Ajing Maluk, 40, is the wife of Majok Alou. They come from Tonga district, south-west of Malakal, the capital of Upper Nile region. Her husband used to fish while she and the children looked after the cattle.

Following a clash between government forces and SPLA troops, Maluk, her husband and four of their children fled to Khartoum in 1984. They left two of their children behind; Maluk is not sure whether they are still alive. She also lost 37 cows which were looted by the government-supported movement, Anya-Nya II. Two years later, two of her brothers died of starvation in Malakal.

Maluk's husband is 57 years old and sick. He and their children are totally dependent on her local beer business. But that business is barely keeping her family alive. The police raid Hilat Shook and other places in Khartoum in search of alcoholic drinks: making, transporting, storing and consuming alcohol are banned.

Maluk says the police always fine her up to £S500 (US$125) on the spot and pocket the money as a bribe. They pour away her brew and often jail her for at least a month.

Another problem for Maluk is the language. She says she always has a lot of problems in the hospital because both she and her husband know only Shilluk, while the doctors and nurses speak only Arabic: they have to guess what is wrong with her sick husband. She is convinced that the drugs they prescribe are not the correct ones.

Motor accidents are also worrying Maluk. She says that a lot of people staying at Hilat Shook have died in car accidents while out on the streets looking for food. Most of them have not really seen vehicles before. She is particularly worried about her own children.

She wants to return to southern Sudan as soon as the war comes to an end.

Abuk Mabek Chol, 29, is a Dinka from Abyei area of southern Kordofan. She used to keep a small sorghum field while her husband, Deng Akot Majok, took care of the cattle. In 1985, her husband went away to Diein, in Darfur province, working as a labourer at the Railway Corporation. While he was away, she was captured by a Rezeigat militiaman.

The next thing she heard about her husband was that he had been killed in the Diein massacre in March 1987: over 1,000 Dinka tribesmen were killed by horse-mounted Rezeigat militiamen.

She had to marry the Rezeigat man and had a daughter, in addition to the two boys she had already from the late Akot. But at her new husband's home she had too much work, for which she and her two sons got little food. Chol fled to Khartoum.

She now stays at Hilat Shook with her three children. She prepares peanuts which she sells on the streets of Khartoum and near cinema halls. But the peanut business does not bring in enough money.

She has been thinking of branching into the more lucrative beer business and tried it in the last week of June 1988. But the experience was bad for her: she was arrested and spent a whole week at the police station because she couldn't produce the bribe which the arresting policeman asked for.

Thirteen hours of rain

The plight of the people of Hilat Shook, and that of almost all the other people displaced by the war, grew still worse on Thursday, 4 August, 1988. That was when more than 20 centimetres (8 inches) of rain fell without a break over 13 hours. It was eight times as much rain as the city received in the whole of 1987 and twice as much as in any whole year for 30 years.

This is how the crisis became known to the world, as reported in newspapers in London:

August 8:

More than a million people were reported to be homeless and scores drowned after torrential rain caused widespread flooding in Khartoum and surrounding provinces ... The capital was cut off

Jeremy Hartley/Panos Pictures

from the rest of the world, with communications down and power lines washed away. There were reports of people being electrocuted as pylons toppled into the water. Thousands are left in the open with no immediate prospect of shelter ... Aid agencies braced themselves for an epidemic of illnesses caused by water contamination. — *The Times*

August 9:

In Khartoum, more than 1.5 million of its 4 million people are without food and shelter, according to government officials and diplomats ... The city has been without power for five days. Most areas have no fresh water. The only link with the outside world is by radio telephone ... The government has declared a state of emergency. — *The Independent*

August 10:

Many of the mud houses in Khartoum have been washed away ... Health authorities warned yesterday of the danger of epidemics of cholera and typhoid ... Refugees from the war in the south living in shanty towns around Khartoum are among the worst-hit. Their plastic, cardboard and mud huts were swept away by the floods which at their peak covered parts of the city with over three feet of water. — *Financial Times*

Khartoum is in "half-gloom", its people threatened with famine and its streets flooded, according to the Egyptian news agency Mena. There are also said to be fires in parts of the city. The reports painted an apocalyptic picture of the capital. — *The Independent*

August 11:

The rains have stopped, but well over three-quarters of Khartoum's residential area is still under water. People who have lost homes and possessions are camping in sports stadiums and more durable buildings on high ground. — *The Guardian*

As the devastating floods spread to wide areas of northern and western Sudan yesterday, Martin Klir, 25, a hotel waiter, described how his pregnant wife and their two children watched the destruction of their home in Omdurman the day the rain came down. "She told me she heard screams and loud noises. So she took the children out and stood helplessly to watch the entire house go further and further until it plunged into the river. We lost everything ... " — *The Independent*

Fears that a second phase of flooding is about to strike rose yesterday as relief workers struggled to avert outbreaks of typhoid, cholera and dysentery among hundreds of thousands of people still without shelter a week after the first disaster. — *The Times*

Jeremy Hartley/Panos Pictures

Jeremy Hartley/Panos Pictures

August 13:

Six weeks ago, Arayak, a 31-year-old Nuer tribesman, took to the road out of desperation born of famine and war in his region in south Sudan. He walked for 28 days before arriving in Khartoum, a human bag of bones, six foot (1.8 metres) tall and weighing no more than seven stone (44 kilograms). Within days of his arrival, the mud shanty in which he was staying in Khartoum was washed away in the rains. But Arayak, like most Sudanese, is not one to despair. What his friends wrought from earth, he can help them build again.
— *The Daily Telegraph*

August 14:

The rain has destroyed an estimated 80,000 buildings in the capital, far more than first reports estimated ... Khartoum is not the only disaster area. A state of emergency has also been declared in Showak and Kasala to the east and at El Damer in the north. But nobody is quite sure what is happening in the rest of the country ... Flying to the north we saw fields on which villagers depend for food covered in water. The railway town of Shendi, through which relief supplies should be passing, was cut off, its railtrack covered with sand as high as a house. At Atbara, 240 kilometres (150 miles) to the north, we found a desolate, apparently deserted city. In Khartoum, there has been rioting by day and a silent blackness by night, punctuated by the fires which have broken out in the city ... Food stocks are quickly dwindling because the floods have cut the roads leading into the city. Lorries find the going difficult, often impossible, even if they can find fuel..An official of the World Health Organization warned: "Khartoum is a time-bomb. Unless drugs are distributed soon, and people inoculated to counter possible epidemics from cholera and typhoid, the situation will soon become critical." Even for Sudan this is a calamity on a monumental scale. — *The Sunday Times*

August 15:

Conditions in the shanty towns which ring Khartoum are still desperately squalid. In Mayo, half an hour's drive away through deep mud, people are living on tiny islands in stagnant water. "These people have not had access to clean water for over a week," said John Patel of Save the Children Fund. "They are using it for

Jeremy Hartley/Panos Pictures

cooking and they seem to be drinking it as well. There is widespread evidence that children are getting diarrhoea. — *The Guardian*

The Nile waters overflowed south of Khartoum yesterday, submerging the surrounding land up to the treetops and adding to the damage already caused ... a government minister says the floods killed 58 people, injured 213 and destroyed 167,000 homes in the Khartoum area. The fresh flooding is threatening to hamper efforts by relief officials to help the two million Sudanese already left homeless after nearly 10 days of flooding ... Renewed rains on Saturday washed away more houses of unbaked mud in the sprawling settlements ringing Khartoum, leaving vast pools of water throughout the capital. — *The Times*

The city of Omdurman looks as if it has been struck by the opposite of a neutron bomb. The type of saturation bombing which struck every square inch of it has destroyed at least 80% of the buildings but, for the time being, left nearly all the people alive. Their technical term for this form of attack is "rain". It reduced Omdurman to mud because it is made of mud ... Most of the roads are made of mud too. Over the mud lies a layer of human beings, goats, sheep, donkeys, excrement, rubbish, vehicles and warm, dirty water. The first cases of typhoid have been reported. There are far more people in need than can possibly receive help ... In the worst state of all, perhaps, are the those displaced by the wars in their squatter camps on the further edges of the district. They had no houses to lose, but their present dwellings do not deserve the name of hovel. — *The Independent*

August 16:

Clean water in the shanty towns around Khartoum is almost non-existent. When available it can cost £S30 (US$ 7.50) a barrel. Elementary sewers have been destroyed, creating stagnant, infested pools. The mosquito population is said to have increased 20-fold, bringing an increased risk of malaria and cholera. — *The Guardian*

A locust plague of biblical proportions is amassing in Sudan ... The rains, which caused the Nile to burst its banks, also created ideal breeding conditions for locusts. — *The Times*

Jeremy Hartley/Panos Pictures

August 17:

The Sudan People's Liberation Army (SPLA) said yesterday that floods had made hundreds of thousands of people homeless in the war-torn south of the country. Radio SPLA listed 10 rebel-held towns seriously hit by flooding, they said some villages were buried under six feet of water and thousands of cattle, sheep and goats had drowned. — *The Independent*

As the Nile continued to rise, Khartoum braced itself for a potentially much more serious second phase of flooding, and details of previously unreported severe problems outside the capital began to filter through. Mark Duffield of Oxfam said that there were reports of 200 people drowned and 1,000 families made homeless by a flash flood at South Geneina in western Sudan. Another charity reported that a fifth of the population of Shoak in eastern Sudan had been affected, many losing their homes and possessions. — *The Times*

August 18:

While the residents of Khartoum try to salvage their possessions, in the south of the country it is civil war as usual. One reason the army has not managed to get relief supplies into Khartoum's slums is that most of its resources are deployed in the south, beating back the encroaching SPLA ... Meanwhile, southerners are still arriving in the north, and there is no let-up in the famine. "There are still more people dying of starvation and deprivation in other parts of Sudan than in Khartoum," says one diplomat. Reports from the border between north and south suggest that as many as 50 people a day may be dying of starvation. — *The Guardian*

Sudanese authorities, nervously watching the flooding Nile, began evacuating thousands of people from two threatened areas of Khartoum yesterday. — *The Daily Telegraph*

August 19:

Health officials have been working non-stop to warn hundreds of thousands of people about the dangers of collecting water from pools of rainwater contaminated by sewage ... In Khartoum yesterday, thousands of men, women and children laboured under a scorching sun to build up the banks of the Nile against the rising water. — *The Independent*

Jeremy Hartley/Panos Pictures

August 22:

Volunteers raced to build flood barriers in Khartoum yesterday as the rising Nile inundated large areas of north and central Sudan. Flood waters roared through similar defences erected in Karima, 335 kilometres (210 miles) to the north-west. Reports said the whole city was under water, apart from a small island. Entire neighbourhoods were swept away in the rich farmland region. Thousands of people were homeless and damage to crops was widespread ... Sudan is also battling with at least 40 swarms of invading desert locusts. — *The Guardian*

August 29:

This emergency is among the most difficult we have experienced. In Khartoum, electricity, water, telephones, roads and rail have all been cut ... It is impossible to guess the scale of the disaster outside Khartoum and in particular the flooded and war-torn south. And flood relief supplies will not address the longer-term emergency caused by war, under-development and debt to the West ... Aid sent so far is being put to good use, saving thousands, if not tens of thousands, of lives. But it is still a drop in the ocean of needs ...
Letter from Christian Aid, London, in *The Independent*

Jeremy Hartley/Panos Pictures

August 31:

Reports came from aid workers in Khartoum yesterday that southerners fleeing drought, war and floods are dying in their thousands. Corpses, many of them children's, litter the roads and railway track leading from the south. The World Food Programme says about 100 people a day are dying in Aweil and about 50 in El Meirem, both towns on the refugee road to the north. — *The Independent*

The governor of Equatoria province reported yesterday that tens of thousand of people were on the move to escape the flooding. He said the worst-affected area was the district of Torit, where absolutely no food remained... Reports filtering through from relief agencies suggested the situation was equally bad, or worse, in other parts...It was estimated that up to 300 people were dying of starvation daily in the country as a whole. — *The Guardian*

Thousands of people have starved to death in the southern Kordofan region in an unpublicised crisis far more urgent than the flood disaster in Khartoum, say relief workers who have just returned from the area ... Miss Cathy Hennessey, of the Irish aid agency, Concern, who until ten days ago was running a feeding centre in the town of el Muglad, south-west of Khartoum, says at least 15 people were dying in her camp every day. "Adults are dropping like flies and children have sores all over their bodies and their bones are sticking out of their skins. Grown men were crawling into camp, diarrhoea literally pouring out of them. You could go along the road and see dead babies lying along the side." ... Most of the people who have died or are at risk are Dinka tribespeople who have fled north, mainly from the region of Bahr el Ghazal. — *The Daily Telegraph*

Jeremy Hartley/Panos Pictures

Background to events

1820: Egyptian military occupation begins unification of Sudan.

1881: Sudanese Islamic leader Mohammed Ahmed ibn Abdallah declares himself Mahdi or "chosen one"; launches crusade to restore Islam.

1882: British occupy Egypt; lead Egyptian troops to march against the Mahdi.

1885: Khartoum taken by forces of Mahdi.

1898: Britain invades Sudan; defeats Mahdist army at battle of Omdurman.

1899: Britain establishes Anglo-Egyptian Condominium, effectively British rule.

1910: British cut off south from northern influence: encourage Christian missionaries, discourage traders, withdraw northern troops. Minimal services or construction work provided in south. Plan to split country and incorporate south into federation of East African states as buffer against spread of Islam.

1920s: Indirect rule established, involving "native administration": recognises certain tribal chiefs, sets up tribal courts under their control.

1930s: Pressures for Sudanese independence grow, forcing Britain to re-examine its intentions.

1940s: Southerners not represented at talks which begin independence process.

1955: First signs of military conflict. Southern troops ordered to the north to attend parade without weapons: mutiny. Persuaded to lay down arms, but several massacres of southerners follow. Rebellion grows as northern troops sent south.
Election of all-Sudanese parliament.

1956: Independence declared.

1958: Rising economic and political problems. Military coup: General Abboud suspends constitution, appoints military rulers for provinces.

Early -1960s: First southern exile party, Sudan African National Union, formed by students and junior administrators who have fled abroad. Organise guerilla army from remnants of 1955 mutineers and new student recruits; known as Anyanya.

1964: Anyanya active in Equatoria province. SANU fighting for right of self-determination for south, with independence as ultimate goal.
Internal dissent, escalating civil war, strikes, poor economic performance. Abboud hands over power to transitional government of radical groups that led resistance to military rule.

1965: All-party Round Table to discuss southern problem; fails to agree formula. Main northern parties insist on unitary national government with no single southern regional government. Southern parties want united southern region.

1968: Elections to constituent assembly which is to draft permanent constitution. Deep divisions: should Sudan have Islamic constitution and laws? Southern delegates walk out when clear that Muslim majority will not accept southern objections.

1969: Civil war escalates to all three southern provinces. Army officers led by Colonel Jafaar Nimeiri take power in Khartoum. "Revolutionary Command Council" and civilian cabinet suspend constitution, ban political parties, abolish native administration. Radical changes: Nimeiri proposes secular socialist state with regional autonomy for south.

1972: Nearly 1 million have died. Talks with southern rebels brings Addis Ababa peace agreement, creating southern regional structure of elected regional assembly and "high executive council": limited autonomy plus promises of development spending. But Nimeiri's government does not have support of northern political parties.
Constitutional changes to create presidential system of

government. Nimeiri elected president unopposed.

Mid -1970s: More coup attempts, including 1976 Libyan-backed bid led by Sadiq El Mahdi, great-grandson of "chosen one". Nimeiri moves right.

1977: Nimeiri re-elected. National Reconciliation brings Muslim Brothers into government.

1983: Nimeiri re-elected. Single southern region divided into three; weakens previously dominant Dinka tribe. Widening opposition. Islamic law, Sharia, introduced: punishments of flogging for drinking alcohol, hand and foot amputation for theft. Patchily imposed outside capital, but unites south in condemnation.
Rebels and mutinous army units meet in Ethiopia. Form Sudan People's Liberation Movement plus armed wing Sudan People's Liberation Army. Colonel John Garang elected chairman of SPLM and commander of SPLA.

1984: Nimeiri imposes state of emergency for five months. Announces he wants Islamic constitution: this is never enacted.

1985: Strikes and riots over political situation and IMF-imposed end to subsidies on basic foods and petrol.
Army takes over while Nimeiri in United States. Establishes one-year interim government of "transitional military council" under General Swared Dahab. Effectively suspends Sharia, but does not abolish it. Southern rebels reject ceasefire.

1986: Meeting arranged at Koka Dam outside Addis Ababa. SPLM insists that it will not discuss southern problem in isolation from issue of unequal regional development throughout country.

Elections: Thirty-seven southern constituencies cannot be contested because of war. Sadiq El Mahdi becomes Prime Minister and Defence Minister in coalition government which includes five southern parties.
Sadiq and Garang meet in Addis Ababa. SPLM agree to link lifting of state of emergency to ceasefire. But differences over repeal of Sharia: SPLM want return to secular laws, government insists Sharia be replaced by

"sound" Islamic laws.

War rages; little chance of turning economy round. By June 1988 arrears to IMF alone amount to US$1 billion, more than half world arrears to Fund. Total US$10 billion debt.

1988: Transitional charter published, proposes constitutional conference.

Fighting expands out of southern region into neighbouring Blue Nile, Southern Kordofan and Southern Darfur. Hundreds of thousands of displaced people; districts devastated by war; reports of near-total collapse of rural economy; 300,000 take refuge in neighbouring Ethiopia.

National Islamic Front enters into coalition government, still led by Sadiq el Mahdi.

More than a million displaced people living in squatter camps on outskirts of Khartoum; camps devastated by floods.

FURTHER READING

Abdel Ghaffar, M.A., (ed) *Some Aspects of Pastoral Nomadism in the Sudan*, Khartoum University Press, 1976.

'Abdel Rahim, M., *Imperialism and Nationalism in the Sudan*, Ithaca Press/Khartoum University Press/Atlantic Highlands, 1986.

'Abdel Rahim, M., *The Development of British Policy in the Southern Sudan 1899-1947*, Khartoum, 1968.

Al-Tayeb, G.D., *Forestry and Land Use in the Sudan*, Khartoum University Press, 1972.

Aguda, O., *Arabism and Pan-Arabism in Sudanese Politics*, Journal of Modern African Studies, June 1973.

Beshir, M.O., *The Development of Education in the Sudan 1898-1956*, Khartoum University Press, 1970.

Beshir, M.O., *The Southern Sudan from Conflict to Peace*, The Khartoum Bookshop, 1975.

Beshir, M.O., *The Southern Sudan; Background to Conflict*, Khartoum University Press, 1970.

Due, J.M. & Due, J.F., *Donor Financing of Agricultural Development in the Southern Sudan: Development or Dependency?*, Illinois Agricultural Economics Staff Paper, Series E, Agricultural Economics, No 81 E 180, July 1981.

Fadl Hassan, Y., (ed) *Sudan in Africa*, Khartoum, 1971.

...lt, P.M., *A Modern History of the Sudan*, Weidenfeld & ...olson, 1963.

Middle East Research and Information Project Reports (MERIP) No. 135, Washington DC, September 1985.

Malwal, B., *People & Power in Sudan — the Struggle for National Stability*, Ithaca Press, 1981.

Muraa, R.M., *A Survey of Non-formal Education Programmes for Women in the Southern Region*, Ahfad University College for Women, Omdurman, 1979.

Oesterdiekhoff, P., & Wohlmuth, K., *The 'Breadbasket' is Empty: the Options of Sudanese Development Policy*, Canadian Journal of African Studies (Revue Canadienne des Etudes Africaines), volume 17, no 1, 1983.

Passmore Sanderson, L.M. & Sanderson, N., *Education, Religion & Politics in Southern Sudan 1899-1964*, Ithaca Press/Khartoum University Press, 1981.

Wai, D.M., (ed) *The Southern Sudan: the Problem of National Integration*, Frank Cass, 1973.